Florian Küchler

THE ROLE OF THE EUROPEAN UNION IN MOLDOVA'S TRANSNISTRIA CONFLICT

With a foreword by Christopher Hill

ibidem-Verlag
Stuttgart

Bibliografische Information der Deutschen Nationalbibliothek
Die Deutsche Nationalbibliothek verzeichnet diese Publikation in der
Deutschen Nationalbibliografie; detaillierte bibliografische Daten sind im
Internet über http://dnb.d-nb.de abrufbar.

Bibliographic information published by the Deutsche Nationalbibliothek
Die Deutsche Nationalbibliothek lists this publication in the Deutsche Nationalbibliografie;
detailed bibliographic data are available in the Internet at http://dnb.d-nb.de.

Coverpicture: Symbols of the self-styled "Transnistrian Moldovan Republic" in the courtyard of an
official building in Tiraspol. Photographed by Florian Küchler 2006.

∞

Gedruckt auf alterungsbeständigem, säurefreien Papier
Printed on acid-free paper

ISSN: 1614-3515

ISBN-10: 3-89821-850-3
ISBN-13: 978-3-89821-850-4

© *ibidem*-Verlag
Stuttgart 2008

Alle Rechte vorbehalten

Das Werk einschließlich aller seiner Teile ist urheberrechtlich geschützt. Jede Verwertung
außerhalb der engen Grenzen des Urheberrechtsgesetzes ist ohne Zustimmung des Verlages
unzulässig und strafbar. Dies gilt insbesondere für Vervielfältigungen,
Übersetzungen, Mikroverfilmungen und elektronische Speicherformen sowie die
Einspeicherung und Verarbeitung in elektronischen Systemen.

All rights reserved. No part of this publication may be reproduced, stored in or introduced into a retrieval
system, or transmitted, in any form, or by any means (electronical, mechanical, photocopying, recording or
otherwise) without the prior written permission of the publisher. Any person who does any unauthorized act
in relation to this publication may be liable to criminal prosecution and civil claims for damages.

Printed in Germany

Soviet and Post-Soviet Politics and Society (SPPS) Vol. 78
ISSN 1614-3515

General Editor: Andreas Umland, *Shevchenko University of Kyiv*, umland@stanfordalumni.org

Editorial Assistant: Olena Sivuda, *Dragomanov Pedagogical University of Kyiv*, sivuda@ukrcognita.com.ua

EDITORIAL COMMITTEE*

DOMESTIC & COMPARATIVE POLITICS
Prof. **Ellen Bos**, *Andrássy University of Budapest*
Dr. **Ingmar Bredies**, *Kyiv-Mohyla Academy*
Dr. **Andrey Kazantsev**, *MGIMO (U) MID RF, Moscow*
Dr. **Heiko Pleines**, *University of Bremen*
Prof. **Richard Sakwa**, *University of Kent at Canterbury*
Dr. **Sarah Whitmore**, *Oxford Brookes University*
Dr. **Harald Wydra**, *University of Cambridge*
SOCIETY, CLASS & ETHNICITY
Col. **David Glantz**, *"Journal of Slavic Military Studies"*
Dr. **Rashid Kaplanov**, *Russian Academy of Sciences*
Dr. **Marlène Laruelle**, *EHESS, Paris*
Dr. **Stephen Shulman**, *Southern Illinois University*
Prof. **Stefan Troebst**, *University of Leipzig*
POLITICAL ECONOMY & PUBLIC POLICY
Prof. em. **Marshall Goldman**, *Wellesley College, Mass.*
Dr. **Andreas Goldthau**, *Stiftung Wissenschaft und Politik*
Dr. **Robert Kravchuk**, *University of North Carolina*
Dr. **David Lane**, *University of Cambridge*
Dr. **Carol Leonard**, *University of Oxford*

Dr. **Maria Popova**, *McGill University, Montreal*
FOREIGN POLICY & INTERNATIONAL AFFAIRS
Dr. **Peter Duncan**, *University College London*
Dr. **Taras Kuzio**, *George Washington University, DC*
Prof. **Gerhard Mangott**, *University of Innsbruck*
Dr. **Diana Schmidt**, *University of Bremen*
Dr. **Lisbeth Tarlow**, *Harvard University, Cambridge*
Dr. **Christian Wipperfürth**, *N-Ost Network, Berlin*
Dr. **William Zimmerman**, *University of Michigan*
HISTORY, CULTURE & THOUGHT
Dr. **Catherine Andreyev**, *University of Oxford*
Prof. **Mark Bassin**, *University of Birmingham*
Dr. **Alexander Etkind**, *University of Cambridge*
Dr. **Gasan Gusejnov**, *University of Bremen*
Prof. em. **Walter Laqueur**, *Georgetown University*
Prof. **Leonid Luks**, *Catholic University of Eichstaett*
Dr. **Olga Malinova**, *Russian Academy of Sciences*
Dr. **Andrei Rogatchevski**, *University of Glasgow*
Dr. **Mark Tauger**, *West Virginia University*
Dr. **Stefan Wiederkehr**, *DHI, Warsaw*

ADVISORY BOARD*

Prof. **Dominique Arel**, *University of Ottawa*
Prof. **Jörg Baberowski**, *Humboldt University of Berlin*
Prof. **Margarita Balmaceda**, *Seton Hall University*
Dr. **John Barber**, *University of Cambridge*
Prof. **Timm Beichelt**, *European University Viadrina*
Prof. **Archie Brown**, *University of Oxford*
Dr. **Vyacheslav Bryukhovetsky**, *Kyiv-Mohyla Academy*
Prof. **Timothy Colton**, *Harvard University, Cambridge*
Prof. **Paul D'Anieri**, *University of Kansas, Lawrence*
Dr. **Heike Dörrenbächer**, *DGO, Berlin*
Dr. **John Dunlop**, *Hoover Institution, Stanford, California*
Dr. **Sabine Fischer**, *EU Institute for Security Studies*
Dr. **Geir Flikke**, *NUPI, Oslo*
Prof. **Alexander Galkin**, *Russian Academy of Sciences*
Prof. **Frank Golczewski**, *University of Hamburg*
Dr. **Nikolas Gvosdev**, *"The National Interest," DC*
Prof. **Mark von Hagen**, *Arizona State University*
Dr. **Guido Hausmann**, *Trinity College Dublin*
Prof. **Dale Herspring**, *Kansas State University*
Dr. **Stefani Hoffman**, *Hebrew University of Jerusalem*
Prof. **Mikhail Ilyin**, *MGIMO (U) MID RF, Moscow*
Prof. **Vladimir Kantor**, *Higher School of Economics*
Dr. **Ivan Katchanovski**, *University of Toronto*
Prof. em. **Andrzej Korbonski**, *University of California*
Dr. **Iris Kempe**, *Center for Applied Policy Research*
Prof. **Herbert Küpper**, *Institut für Ostrecht München*
Dr. **Rainer Lindner**, *Stiftung Wissenschaft und Politik*
Dr. **Vladimir Malakhov**, *Russian Academy of Sciences*
Dr. **Luke March**, *University of Edinburgh*

Dr. **Michael McFaul**, *Stanford University, California*
Prof. **Birgit Menzel**, *University of Mainz-Germersheim*
Prof. **Valery Mikhailenko**, *The Urals State University*
Prof. **Emil Pain**, *Higher School of Economics, Moscow*
Dr. **Oleg Podvintsev**, *Russian Academy of Sciences*
Prof. **Olga Popova**, *St. Petersburg State University*
Dr. **Alex Pravda**, *University of Oxford*
Dr. **Erik van Ree**, *University of Amsterdam*
Dr. **Joachim Rogall**, *Robert Bosch Foundation, Stuttgart*
Prof. **Peter Rutland**, *Wesleyan University, Middletown*
Dr. **Sergei Ryabov**, *Kyiv-Mohyla Academy*
Prof. **Marat Salikov**, *The Urals State Law Academy*
Dr. **Gwendolyn Sasse**, *University of Oxford*
Prof. **Jutta Scherrer**, *EHESS, Paris*
Prof. **Robert Service**, *University of Oxford*
Mr. **James Sherr**, *Defence Academy of the UK, Swindon*
Dr. **Oxana Shevel**, *Tufts University, Medford*
Prof. **Eberhard Schneider**, *University of Siegen*
Prof. **Olexander Shnyrkov**, *Shevchenko University, Kyiv*
Prof. **Hans-Henning Schröder**, *University of Bremen*
Prof. **Viktor Shnirelman**, *Russian Academy of Sciences*
Dr. **Lisa Sundstrom**, *University of British Columbia*
Dr. **Philip Walters**, *"Religion, State and Society," Leeds*
Prof. **Zenon Wasyliw**, *Ithaca College, New York State*
Dr. **Lucan Way**, *University of Toronto*
Dr. **Markus Wehner**, *"Frankfurter Allgemeine Zeitung"*
Dr. **Andrew Wilson**, *University College London*
Prof. **Jan Zielonka**, *University of Oxford*
Prof. **Andrei Zorin**, *University of Oxford*

* While the Editorial Committee and Advisory Board support the General Editor in the choice and improvement of manuscripts for publication, responsibility for remaining errors and misinterpretations in the series' volumes lies with the books' authors.

Soviet and Post-Soviet Politics and Society (SPPS)
ISSN 1614-3515

Founded in 2004 and refereed since 2007, SPPS makes available affordable English-, German- and Russian-language studies on the history of the countries of the former Soviet bloc from the late Tsarist period to today. It publishes approximately 20 volumes per year, and focuses on issues in transitions to and from democracy such as economic crisis, identity formation, civil society development, and constitutional reform in CEE and the NIS. SPPS also aims to highlight so far understudied themes in East European studies such as right-wing radicalism, religious life, higher education, or human rights protection. The authors and titles of previously published and forthcoming manuscripts are listed at the end of this book. For a full description of the series and reviews of its books, see http://www.ibidem-verlag.de/red/spps.

Note for authors (as of 2007): After successful review, fully formatted and carefully edited electronic master copies of up to 250 pages will be published as b/w A5 paperbacks and marketed in Germany (e.g. vlb.de, buchkatalog.de, amazon.de). English-language books will, in addition, be marketed internationally (e.g. amazon.com). For longer books, formatting/editorial assistance, different binding, oversize maps, coloured illustrations and other special arrangements, authors' fees between €100 and €1500 apply. Publication of German doctoral dissertations follows a separate procedure. Authors are asked to provide a high-quality electronic picture on the object of their study for the book's front-cover. Younger authors may add a foreword from an established scholar. Monograph authors and collected volume editors receive two free as well as further copies for a reduced authors' price, and will be asked to contribute to marketing their book as well as finding reviewers and review journals for them. These conditions are subject to yearly review, and to be modified, in the future. Further details at www.ibidem-verlag.de/red/spps-authors.

Editorial correspondence & manuscripts should, until 2008, be sent to: Dr. Andreas Umland, DAAD, German Embassy, vul. Bohdana Khmelnitskoho 25, UA-01901 Kiev, Ukraine; umland@stanfordalumni.org.

Business correspondence & review copy requests should be sent to: *ibidem*-Verlag, Julius-Leber-Weg 11, D-30457 Hannover, Germany; tel.: +49(0)511-2622200; fax: +49(0)511-2622201; spps@ibidem-verlag.de.

Book orders & payments should be made via the publisher's electronic book shop at: http://www.ibidem-verlag.de/red/SPPS_EN/

Recent Volumes

70 *David Rupp*
Die Rußländische Föderation und die russischsprachige Minderheit in Lettland
Eine Fallstudie zur Anwaltspolitik Moskaus gegenüber den russophonen Minderheiten im „Nahen Ausland" von 1991 bis 2002
Mit einem Vorwort von Helmut Wagner
ISBN 978-3-89821-778-1

71 *Taras Kuzio*
Theoretical and Comparative Perspectives on Nationalism
New Directions in Cross-Cultural and Post-Communist Studies
With a foreword by Paul Robert Magocsi
ISBN 978-3-89821-815-3

72 *Christine Teichmann*
Die Hochschultransformation im heutigen Osteuropa
Kontinuität und Wandel bei der Entwicklung des postkommunistischen Universitätswesens
Mit einem Vorwort von Oskar Anweiler
ISBN 978-3-89821-842-9

73 *Julia Kusznir*
Der politische Einfluss von Wirtschaftseliten in russischen Regionen
Eine Analyse am Beispiel der Erdöl- und Erdgasindustrie, 1992-2005
Mit einem Vorwort von Wolfgang Eichwede
ISBN 978-3-89821-821-4

74 *Alena Vysotskaya*
Russland, Belarus und die EU-Osterweiterung
Zur Minderheitenfrage und zum Problem der Freizügigkeit des Personenverkehrs
Mit einem Vorwort von Katlijn Malfliet
ISBN 978-3-89821-822-1

75 *Heiko Pleines (Hrsg.)*
Corporate Governance in post-sozialistischen Volkswirtschaften
ISBN 978-3-89821-766-8

76 *Stefan Ihrig*
Wer sind die Moldawier?
Rumänismus versus Moldowanismus in Historiographie und Schulbüchern der Republik Moldova, 1991-2006
Mit einem Vorwort von Holm Sundhaussen
ISBN 978-3-89821-466-7

77 *Galina Kozhevnikova in collaboration with Alexander Verkhovsky and Eugene Veklerov*
Ultra-Nationalism and Hate Crimes in Contemporary Russia
The 2004-2006 Annual Reports of Moscow's SOVA Center
With a foreword by Stephen D. Shenfield
ISBN 978-3-89821-868-9

For Mirela, who has herself experienced two terrible conflicts, but never lost her magic smile…

Rezumat (Romanian Abstract)

Integrarea Bulgariei şi României în UE a adus Republica Moldova la porţile Uniunii ca vecin nou şi necunoscut. Atunci ar fi logic să fie adaptate şi discursuri academice şi politice la ultima avansare spre est al frontierei Europene. Totuşi Europa de Vest şi Statele Unite până acum nu au dat multă atenţie Moldovei şi geopoliticii Mării Negre, nici a acţiunilor celuilalt mare actor în zonă: Rusia. Acest fapt este mult mai serios dacă luăm în considerare diviziunile politice serioase şi conflictele nerezolvate în zonă. Unul dintre ele este conflictul transnistrean din Republica Moldova.

Ca o contribuţie pentru agenda cercetării despre Republica Moldova, această carte analizează interesele, poziţia oficială, adevăratul impact şi rolul potenţial al Uniunii Europene în conflictul intern al Republicii Moldova cu separatiştii transnistreni precum şi tensiunile externe cu Federaţia Rusă legate de el. Pentru acest efort, cartea reevaluează şi conflictul transnistrean în sine, precum şi cauzele şi implicaţiile sale. Împotriva propunerilor frecvente, conflictul nu are o bază etnică încât este fondat pe diferitele interese ale elitelor şi „actorilor" geopolitici.

Până acum, Uniunea Europeană nu a fost foarte activă în efortul internaţional de a rezolva conflictul transnistrean şi în relaţiile generale cu Republica Moldova. Totuşi această carte ajunge la concluzia că acum este din ce în ce mai important, mai posibil şi mai probabil că Uniunea Europeană contribuie la rezolvarea conflictului. Însa mult va depinde de relaţiile cu alţi „actori" geopolitici ca Statele Unite şi Rusia şi de acţiunile lor. În sfârşit, cartea oferă recomandării pentru politica viitoare a Uniunii Europene în legătura cu Republica Moldova.

Conţinutul acestei lucrări este bazat şi pe diferite călătorii de cercetare în Republica Moldova, Transnistria şi statele vecine.

Резюме (Russian Abstract)

В результате вступления в Европейский Союз Болгарии и Румынии Молдова, являющаяся новым и малоизвестным соседом Европейского Союза, оказалась на пороге расширенного Союза. В связи с этим очевидно, что в академической сфере, а также в кругах, формирующих национальную и международную политику, должен был бы возникнуть соответствующий интерес к такому расширению пределов Европейской интеграции. Однако Западная Европа и Соединенные Штаты уделили сравнительно мало внимания Молдове и геополитике Черноморского региона, в том числе действиям ещё одного важного игрока в регионе – России. Такое отношение усугубляется еще и существованием в регионе ряда политических разногласий и неразрешенных конфликтов, одним из которых является приднестровский конфликт в Молдове.

В данной книге анализируются интересы, официальная позиция, реальное влияние и потенциальная роль ЕС во внутреннем конфликте Молдовы с сепаратистами Приднестровья и связанное с этим внешнеполитическое напряжение между Молдовой и Россией. Для осуществления этих задач, в книге проводится новый анализ ситуации связанной с Приднестровским конфликтом, его причин и следствий. Вопреки широко распространённому предположению об этническом происхождении конфликта, в книге показано, что это преимущественно конфликт элит и геополитических интересов.

До настоящего времени, роль ЕС в разрешении конфликта и деятельность ЕС в Молдове в целом были довольно ограниченными. Однако выводом данной книги является то, что участие ЕС в разрешении приднестровского конфликта становится всё более важным, при этом возрастают возможности и вероятность активизации такого участия. При этом масштаб действий ЕС в Молдове и Приднестровье будет зависеть от отношений Евросоюза с другими геополитическими игроками, такими как США и Россия. Более того, данная книга предлагает рекомендации для дальнейшей политики ЕС в отношении Молдовы.

В книге используются сведения, собранные автором во время научных поездок в Молдову, Приднестровье и соседние страны.

Contents

Rezumat (Romanian Abstract) 7

Резюме (Russian Abstract) 9

List of Tables, Figures and Pictures 15

Abbreviations and Acronyms 17

Foreword 21

Acknowledgements 23

1 Introduction 27

2 The Transnistria conflict 31

   2.1 A very brief history 31

   2.2 Common misconceptions 33

   2.3 Roots of the conflict 48

3 International conflict resolution efforts 59

   3.1 History 59

   3.2 Actors 63

   3.3 Themes and solutions 75

4	**The EU and Moldova**	81
4.1	Evolution of relations	81
4.2	Agents and agencies	86
4.3	Issues	91
4.4	The EU and the settlement of the Transnistria conflict	98
5	**Conclusions**	103
6	**Recommendations to the EU**	107
7	**Update**	113

Bibliography *115*

Index *139*

List of Tables, Figures and Pictures

Tables

Table 2.1 Key events related to the Transnistria conflict 33

Table 2.2 Ethnicities in Moldova 34

Table 3.1 Key events in the international search for a solution 60

Figures

Figure 1 Map of Moldova, Transnistria and neighbouring countries 25

Pictures

Picture 2.1 Lenin statue in Chişinău 36

Picture 2.2 Statues of A.V. Suvorov and Stephen the Great 37

Picture 2.3 Street sign in Tiraspol 39

Picture 2.4 Transnistrian coat of arms in the streets of Tiraspol 40

Picture 2.5 Honorary citizens of Tiraspol 51

Picture 2.6 Headquaters of the youth movement *Proriv* 53

Picture 2.7 Flags of the Ukrainian *Pora* movement 53

Picture 2.8 The DHL office in Tiraspol 54

Picture 3.1 Supporters of pro-Russian parties in Kyiv 69

Abbreviations and Acronyms

ASSR	Autonomous Soviet Socialist Republic
BSEC	Organisation of Black Sea Economic Cooperation
CFSP	common foreign and security policy
CIS	Commonwealth of Independent States
CoE	Council of Europe
CSCE	Conference on Security and Cooperation in Europe
EBRD	European Bank for Reconstruction and Development
EC	European Community
ECHO	European Community Humanitarian Office
ECHR	European Court of Human Rights
EIB	European Investment Bank
ENP	European Neighbourhood Policy
ENPI	European Neighbourhood and Partnership Instrument
EU	European Union
EUBAM	European Union Border Assistance Mission (to Moldova and Ukraine)
EUSR	European Union Special Representative
fdi	foreign direct investment
FTA	free trade area

GSP	Generalised System of Preferences
GU(U)AM	Georgia, Ukraine, (Uzbekistan,) Azerbaijan, Moldova
IFIs	international financial institutions
MEP	Member of European Parliament
MFN	most-favoured nation
NATO	North Atlantic Treaty Organisation
NGO	Non-Governmental Organisation
NIS	newly independent states
OSCE	Organisation for Security and Cooperation in Europe
PACE	Parliamentary Assembly of the Council of Europe
PCA	Partnership and Cooperation Agreement
PMR	Priednistrovskaya Moldavskaya Respublika (Transnistria)
SSR	Soviet Socialist Republic
TACIS	Technical Assistance to the Commonwealth of Independent States
TBO	TACIS Branch Office
TCA	Trade and Cooperation Agreement
USSR	Union of Soviet Socialist Republics (Soviet Union)
UN	United Nations
US	United States (of America)
UNDP	United Nations Development Programme

Foreword

Florian Küchler has done us all a service by his meticulous research into the important problem of Transnistria. The average citizen of a western European country is unlikely to have heard of Moldova, let alone the conflict which has been boiling on that country's eastern frontier for the past 20 years. And, it might be asked, why should they care in any case? The answer to this is two-fold. Firstly, European citizens have been taught by the experiences of 1939-45, and then again the 1990s in the Balkans, that they run grave moral and practical risks if they ignore the sufferings of peoples in other countries. 'Any man's death diminishes me, because I am involved in mankind' said John Donne in the seventeenth century, and even if we cannot take on responsibility for preventing killing in every part of the world, there is now a presumption that a savage conflict outside our borders must engage our conscience and lead to some kind of constructive effort at resolving it, so as to relieve suffering. This is also because once violence breaks out, even within a single state, but especially across borders, no-one can tell where it will end or where it might lead. The examples of Serbia 1914, Czechoslovakia 1938, Bosnia 1992 and Iraq 2003 are too striking to ignore. When war breaks out in the Lebanon the world immediately takes notice. But less obvious places like Rwanda, Kurdish Iraq – and Transnistria – are also flashpoints and sites of potential slaughter.

Florian is passionately concerned with the fate of Moldova. But he does not allow passion to blind him to the need for informed, cool analysis. He knows the country and has worked hard to acquire the language competence which marks out the expert from the mere commentator. He also has a very good understanding of the European Union's capabilities in external relations, especially in the EU's 'neighbourhood', through his work in the Kiev Delegation. The accession of Bulgaria and Rumania to the EU in 2007 has brought Moldova right up to the Union's borders, and implicated us all much more than before. We should all benefit from finding out much more about Moldova, Transnistria and the geopolitics of the Black Sea region. Florian Küchler's book is an excellent place to start.

Christopher Hill
Centre of International Studies,
University of Cambridge

Acknowledgements

First of all, I wish to acknowledge the invaluable help and advice of my supervisor Professor Christopher Hill. He gave me general guidance as well as constructive feedback on work in progress and has been very forthcoming with flexible arrangements to accommodate my absence from Cambridge due to research and work abroad during most of the preparation time for this work.

Also, I would like to thank all those who – through their helpful comments and critical questions – have pointed me to useful information and contact persons, helped identify possible problems in my approach and suggested alternatives. This applies in particular to my co-students on the "Master of Studies in International Relations" course, my colleagues at the Delegation of the European Commission in Ukraine, where I worked as an intern during the entire writing-up phase and the contributors and audiences of the various conferences that I attended. In the end, however, I would have never turned my master thesis into this book, had it not been for the encouragement I received from Dr. Andreas Umland and an anonymous peer reviewer.

Furthermore, I would like to thank my girlfriend Mirela Glušac for proofreading my Romanian summary, my former colleague Irina Leonenko for her help with the Russian version and the geographers Hanka Poppitz and Tobias Kerschke for ensuring that I was able to include a high quality map of Moldova and Transnistria after I had struggled to get hold of the authors and copyright holders of suitable maps found on the internet.

Last, but by no means least, I am forever indebted to my parents Ursula and Hans-Georg Küchler for their love and unconditional support for my demanding international research and work schedules.

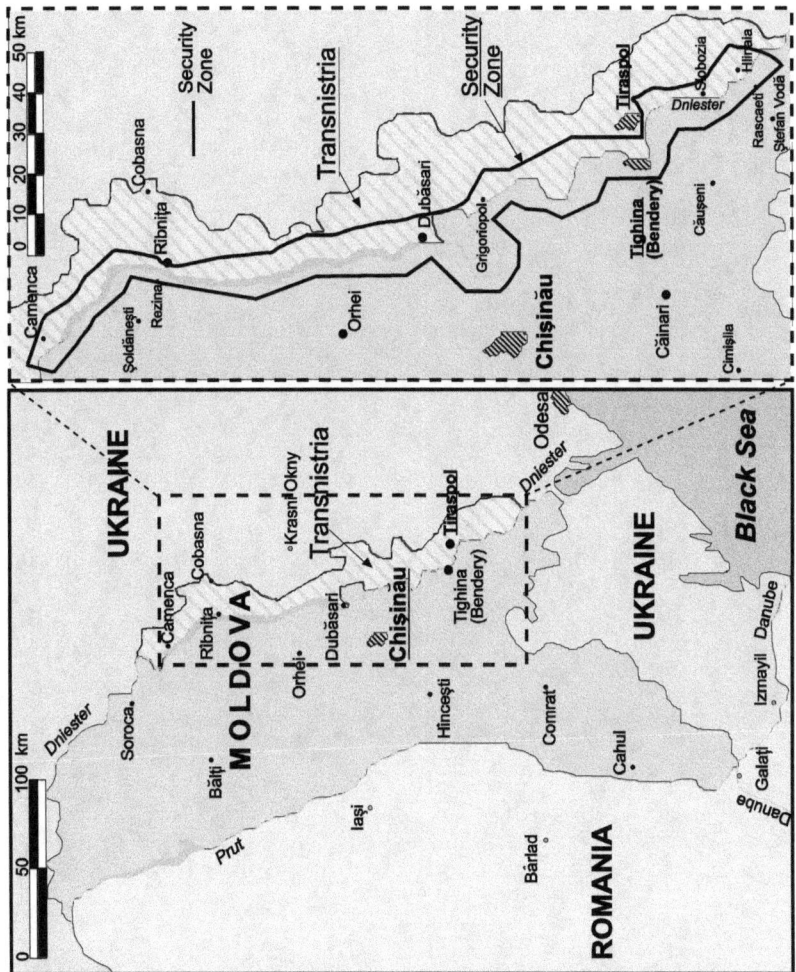

Figure 1 Map of Moldova, Transnistria and neighbouring regions (Author: Hanka Poppitz, Copyright: Florian Küchler)

1 Introduction[1]

On 1 January 2007, Romania and Bulgaria entered the European Union (EU), thus completing the second half of their Euro-Atlantic integration process after their joining NATO in 2004. This concludes the "encirclement" of the former Yugoslav states by EU and NATO members, gives the EU access to the Black Sea and – with Moldova – brings a new neighbour to the doorstep of the enlarged Union. Therefore, it would seem obvious that academic debates as well as policies of national and international actors would have to adapt to the realities of this new periphery.

Yet, whereas Yugoslavia and its successor states have received considerable academic and media attention as a result of the violent conflicts that occurred there in the 1990s, Western Europe and the United States have given comparatively little attention to the EU's Eastern European neighbours and the wider geopolitics of the Black Sea region, including the actions of the other big actor in the region: Russia. Although during the 2004 "Orange Revolution" Ukraine was the recipient of considerable international attention, this was rather short-lived. Moreover, there has not been a significant spill-over effect in terms of increasing interest in other countries such as Moldova, Belarus or Georgia. This is all the more serious if one takes into account the political divisions and conflicts that linger in the area.

Whilst Ukraine witnessed no major violence during its "Orange Revolution", many other places did. Violence and even outright warfare, if small-scale, has swept through several parts of Russia's near abroad

---

[1] This introduction is a partial adaptation of the introduction of a book review written by the author for the Cambridge Review of International Affairs (Küchler, 2007a).

and some of its own border regions.[2] Of course, none of these reached the scale of violence that has accompanied the break-up of Yugoslavia. Moreover, unlike Yugoslavia, most of the conflicts were relatively far away from Western Europe and therefore much lower down the European political agenda. Also, fortunately there is no major fighting on post-Soviet territory at the time of writing. However, many recent conflicts have simply been frozen, rather than resolved, and one does not have to reach beyond the Black Sea for a case study. One of these so-called "frozen conflicts" (Brennan, 2003, p. 1) is that between Moldova and the separatists in its Transnistrian province,[3] who are militarily and economically backed by Russia.

Although, for the time being, this conflict is unlikely to escalate into major violence, the EU has a strong interest in resolving it as soon as possible. This is not only due to the various cross-border problems immediately resulting from the conflict and the illegal activities of the internationally unrecognised Transnistria. Rather, the solution, or not, of the conflict could have much wider implications for the role of the European Union as a regional and global power. This is partially because of its interconnection with other issues such as the recognition of Kosovo's independence, EU-Russian relations and NATO's eastwards expansion.

The aim of this book is to identify the EU's interests in – and its actual and potential role in the resolution of – the Transnistria conflict.

---

[2] During and after the break-up of the Soviet Union, civil wars took place in Chechnya, Nagorno Karabakh, Ingushetia, Ossetia, Abkhazia, Adjaria, Moldova and Tajikistan (Kotkin, 2001, p. 4)

[3] Names of countries and places are a highly politically sensitive subject in the era of post-Soviet nationalism. Therefore, any choice of spellings needs a justification. In this case, the choice of "Moldova" over "Moldavia" can be justified, because the former is the country's own official spelling and is now also widely used outside Russian-speaking countries. Choosing "Transnistria" over the separatists' own spelling as "*Priednistrovje*", reflects common usage in non-Russian literature and media and avoids unintentionally giving legitimacy to the highly problematic regime of the self-styled "republic".
For Ukrainian city names, too, this book adopts the new official Ukrainian spellings instead of the Russian transliterations that are still frequenttly encountered (i.e. "Kyiv" and "Odesa" instead of "Kiev" and "Odessa") and the – now politically correct – usage of "Ukraine" without article.

However, whilst relatively few people are even aware of the conflict's existence, even those who do know about it often see both the causes and implications of the conflict in overly simplistic ways. This is reflected in much of the literature as well as media reports on the topic. Thus, the following sections represent a re-evaluation of conflict itself in which gaps and contradictions in the literature are resolved by the author's own observations from several research field trips to Moldova, Romania, Ukraine and Russia as well as a number of formal and informal interviews. In some cases these measures were even necessary to obtain rather basic information.

This book adopts the views of neither of the two sides. If siding with anyone, the author understands his position as in favour of the European Union as well as the people of Europe (including Moldova and Transnistria), in whose interest the resolution of the Transnistria conflict is. It is meant to be policy oriented in that it analyses the actual policies of the EU with respect to Transnistria, Moldova and the region and also results in a number of policy recommendations and options to be considered by the European Union and its member states.

2 The Transnistria conflict

2.1 A very brief history

History and geography played a great part in the creation of the Transnistria conflict. The two conflicting parties are based in Moldova's two main historical regions: Bessarabia, situated between the rivers Prut and Dniester, and Transnistria, on the left bank of the Dniester. The latter was longer under imperial Russian and Soviet rule than the former, which was acquired only in the early 19th century from the Ottoman Empire, broke away during the Russian civil war in 1918, joined Romania in 1919 and was eventually returned to Moscow through the 1940 Molotov-Ribbentrop Pact. Transnistria, however, had never been part of Romania save for a brief period of occupation during the Second World War. It was originally part of Ukraine, but became the centre of the Moldovan Autonomous Soviet Socialist Republic (ASSR) created by the Soviet Union to emphasize their claim on Bessarabian Moldova (CSCE, 1994). While a part of this Moldovan ASSR was reincorporated into the Ukrainian Soviet Socialist Republic (SSR), present-day Transnistria became part of the Moldovan SSR and hence of today's independent Moldova.

Moldova's passage into sovereign statehood was from the outset opposed by the predominantly Russian elites in Transnistria. In fact, Russian and pro-Russian groups in Transnistria and Gagauzia – an area in Southern Bessarabia that is populated by orthodox Christians of Turkic origin – organised their own movements to counter Moldovan nationalism and independence quicker than the Moldovans (Crowther, 2004a) out of fear of becoming part of Romania and/or being forcibly "Romanianised". At first their *Yedinstvo* (Unity) movement was aiming to preserve the Soviet Union and stay an integral part thereof (Katchanovski, 2006), but when the dismemberment of the Union of Soviet Socialist Republics (USSR) in general and the independence of Moldova in particular seemed unavoidable, they declared their independence from Moldova in 1990, again outrunning the Moldovans, who declared full independence only in 1991 (Fodor, 1995). Gagauzia became the self-styled *Gagauz Yeri* or Gagauz Republic, whereas Transnistria declared itself to be the *Priednistrovskaya Moldavskaya Respublika* (PMR), meaning "On-the-Dniester Moldavian Republic" (Pridnestrovie.net, 2006), thus implying a claim of parts of the right bank of the Dniester in addition to historic Transnistria.

Naturally, these moves alienated the Moldovan government which saw its sovereignty and therefore its newly acquired statehood under threat. However, initially no consolidated crackdown campaign was launched against the separatists, probably because the Moldovan government was still too inexperienced and lacked resources (Laitin, 1998, p. 330). Nonetheless, clashes occurred between Moldovan police forces and separatist paramilitary forces, who step-by-step seized all official buildings and public institutions in Transnistria, often meeting only unarmed resistance by Moldovan peasants (CSCE, 1994, p. 2).

Eventually, it was the Transnistrian side, which escalated the conflict, by crossing the Dniester to take control of the Bessarabian town of Tighina/Bendery, a strategic bridgehead opposite the Transnistrian capital Tiraspol. The Moldovan government responded by sending troops and volunteers, and fierce street fighting – including the use of heavy armaments – followed (Teague, 2004). Over 1,000 people are said to have died in this hot phase of the conflict, over 5,000 were wounded and more than 100,000 became refugees (Ozhiganov, 1997, pp. 145-146).

The Transnistrians prevailed relatively quickly, because they had the tacit – and sometimes even active – support of the Russian 14th Army that remained in Moldova after the collapse of the Soviet Union (Gherman, 2003, p. 183). In fact, they most likely only chose to escalate the conflict once they had been assured of Russian support for their cause. Table 2.1 summarises the key events in the build-up, hot phase and aftermath of the Transnistria conflict.

Table 2.1 Key events related to the Transnistria conflict

Date		Event
1986		Seventh Party Congress of the Communist Party of the Soviet Union – Gorbachev announces *perestroika*
1988		*Yedinstvo* (Unity) movement founded in Transnistria
1989		Formation of the Moldovan Popular Front
1990	February	First Democratic elections in the Moldovan SSR
	June	Moldova declares sovereignty
	August	Gagauzia declares independence
	September	Transnistria declares independence
1991		Moldova declares complete independence from the Soviet Union
1992	March	Moldovan government declares state of emergency
	May	Full-scale civil war between Moldovan government and Transnistrian separatists *(Hot phase)*
	July	Cease-fire agreement signed by Moldovan president Snegur and Russian president Yeltsin (!)
1993		Moldovan parliament refuses to approve a strengthening of the CIS
1994		Moldova and Russia sign an agreement on the withdrawal of Russian troops, subsequently ratified only by the Moldovan side
1995		Russian 14th Army in Moldova is downgraded to the level of an operational group

(Fodor, 1995; Ionescu, 2002)

2.2 Common misconceptions

The Transnistria conflict is most commonly described as an ethnic conflict, and at first sight – for example after reading through the brief history above – it may seem logical to place it into this category. There is no immediately apparent reason, why the underlying factors of this conflict should be any different from those of other ethnic conflicts involving violent shifts in the relationships between two or more ethnic groups. Therefore, a discussion of ethnicity and related factors in Moldova is unavoidable:

Moldova unquestionably is a multi-ethnic, multi-national and multi-linguistic state. Whilst ethnicity and nationality are contested concepts and often difficult to pin down, in Moldova's case it is clear that the different groups' culture and languages are both sufficiently different from one another and similar to their ethnic kin in other established (nation) states to meaningfully speak of ethnicity and national groups. They merely share a common state out of historical circumstance and do not have a common cultural and linguistic heritage comparable to that of the Serbo-Croatian speakers of former Yugoslavia.

In both Bessarabia and Transnistria ethnic Romanians make up the majority of the population, although in the latter region they only form a plurality. Table 2.2 shows the regional variations in the proportions of the main ethnic groups of the Moldovan population. However, Moldovan population statistics are generally unreliable, as the last census was only carried out in Bessarabia, whereas the last one conducted in the whole country dates back to 1989. Moreover, it is estimated that up to one quarter of the workforce is currently working abroad (Hensel & Gudîm, 2004, p. 90), legally and illegally, due to the country's severe economic problems. Nonetheless, the numbers of the 1989 Soviet census would seem the most appropriate ones, as they can be taken as an approximation of the situation before the outbreak of the conflict. Although there have been some changes in these proportions as a result of the Transnistria conflict, no large-scale ethnic cleansing has taken place (International Crisis Group, 2006, p. 1). Therefore, today's proportions are likely to be similar, whilst absolute numbers would reflect economic immigration.

Table 2.2 Ethnicities in Moldova

	All of Moldova	Transnistria
Romanians	65%	40%
Ukrainians	14%	28%
Russians	13%	25%
Gagauz	4%	1%
Bulgarians	2%	2%
Others	2%	4%
Based on 1989 numbers (Fodor, 1995)		

To avoid confusion between ethnicity and citizenship, in this book the term "Romanian" is used to denote the dominant ethnic or national group in Moldova, with linguistic and cultural ties to Romania, whereas "Moldovan" is used to refer to all the citizens of Moldova, which thus includes ethnic Russians, Ukrainians, Gagauz and others. Seen objectively, Moldovan and Romanian are virtually the same languages, and the two groups are ethnically and culturally extremely similar, if not the same. Within Moldova, however, there is a debate over the existence of a separate Moldovan ethnic group and language and hence a separate Moldovan nation (King, 2000, p. 10). Therefore, in some texts the term "Moldovan" is used to denote the ethnic group termed "Romanian" here, making other citizens of Moldova hyphenated Moldovans. However, the purpose of such a usage is not merely to internally elevate the status of Romanian Moldovans by reducing other ethnicities to foreign elements. Rather, calling Moldova's Romanians "Moldovans" is evidence of the simultaneously occurring nation-building and state-building processes in the country and serves external, as well as internal purposes.

The debate over a separate Moldovan identity actually originated in the late Russian Empire's and Soviet rulers' attempts to artificially move Moldovans into the Slav category of peoples and languages thus emphasizing the difference of Moldovans from neighbouring Romanians to counter sympathies for any plans of (re)creating a greater Romania (King, 1995, p. 4). However, up to the present, a substantial proportion of Romanian Moldovans has upheld this view (Meurs, 2002, p. 417). Whilst even these so-called "Moldovanists" have given up the Cyrillic script that had been imposed by Moscow to distinguish Moldovan from Romanian (see picture 2.1), they do continue the tradition of writing distorted history textbooks and even published a Romanian-Moldovan dictionary (Stati, 2003), causing outrage amongst many of their fellow compatriots and of course in Romania (Dungaciu, 2005b). In essence, these are bold efforts in carving out a separate Moldovan national identity to justify Moldova's nationhood vis-à-vis other states. One must not forget that all three of the major ethnic groups in Moldova represent existing nations, based in states which have potential or even actual irredentist claims to some or all of the country. After all, Moldovans share their languages, cultures and even national heroes with these states (see picture 2.2).

Picture 2.1 Lenin statue in Chişinău with Cyrillic Romanian and Russian inscriptions

Closely related to ethnicity, are a whole range of language issues: Not only is there a debate about the name and nature of Moldova's main language, but there are also debates about the roles of the various minority languages that make Moldova a polyglot country. Although Ukrainians are the second largest ethnic group, actually Russian is the second most common mother tongue. This is, because large proportions of the Ukrainians and many members of other ethnic groups – including some Romanians – have been assimilated through the long history of Russian and Soviet rule (Zaporojan-Pirgari, 2004, p. 65). Of the smaller communities, the Gagauz, Bulgarians and Roma to some extent preserved their own languages whilst generally also speaking Russian and/or Romanian, whereas the few remaining Jews speak mostly Russian (Zaporojan-Pirgari, 2004, pp. 66-67).

The official language of state is "Moldovan", but many people and even the national anthem refer to it simply as *limba noastră* meaning "our language" thus avoiding the Romanian vs. Moldovan debate (King, 2000, p. 159). Additionally, Russian has been given a special status as the "language of interethnic communication", and Gagauz is an official language within the Gagauz autonomy (Crowther, 1997a, p. 341). However, Russian unofficially still dominates in many areas of public life and has been reintroduced as a compulsory school subject (Waters, 2002).

The media landscape provides a good example of this domination: Whilst Moldovan state TV channels mainly broadcast in Romanian, with only special slots for Russian language programmes, a wide array of private Russian TV channels exists. These often have financial backing from Russia and/or are direct rebroadcasts of Russian programmes, having at their disposal a wide selection of existing Russian or dubbed international material. This makes them a preferred option across ethnic boundaries vis-à-vis the inferior Romanian programming that generates

Picture 2.2 Statues of A.V. Suvorov (18th century Russian gerneral and founder of Tiraspol) and Stephen the Great (15th century prince of Moldavia) in Tiraspol and Chişinău respectively, both representing national heroes that are shared with other countries (Russia and Romania)

much less material and relies mainly on subtitles for international films and shows. Radio stations and the newspaper market to a large extent mirror this situation. Most radio stations ignore the legal requirement for keeping two-thirds of broadcasting in Romanian, and newspaper kiosks display predominantly Russian language print-media (Clej & Canţîr, 2004, p. 58).

Moreover, Russians always tended to live more in the cities whereas the countryside was predominantly populated by Romanian (and Ukrainian) peasants. Whilst Moldovan peasants with a poor knowledge of Russian no longer have the problems of bygone eras when they were often literally not understood in the Russian-dominated cities, Russian remains a key business language. This applies not just to the area of foreign trade that is traditionally directed towards the countries of the Commonwealth of Independent States (CIS). Even representatives of international organisations, foreign diplomats and embassy employees in Moldova often speak only or mainly Russian, a situation that mirrors much of neighbouring Ukraine.[4]

Considering this unofficial domination of Russian, it is not surprising that generally Moldova's ethnic Romanians speak Russian a lot better than their Russian counterparts speak Romanian. Russians can afford not to learn Romanian well, whereas Romanians would have a lot to lose if they didn't learn the language that plays so many important if unofficial roles in their country. In any case, most Romanians learn Russian at school and through everyday interethnic contacts, and in the author's experience, surprisingly few have strong antipathies against this language. This is also reflected in people's private lives in that mixed marriages often result in predominantly Russian speaking families, and even purely Romanian families switch back and forth between Romanian and

---

[4] The author has himself come across many such cases. In the Chişinău he was surprised to find staff of the local Ukrainian embassy's consular section speaking only Russian and English, but neither their own country's, nor the host country's official state languages. For a criticism of Western diplomats in Moldova speaking only Russian and signing official documents in Cyrillic script, see Dungaciu (2005b).

Russian in their casual home conversations. In recent years, however, there is a growing tendency towards more equal relations between the two languages, since Russians are now beginning to make efforts to learn Romanian and increasingly also send their children to schools teaching in Romanian (Dima, 2001, p. 149; Nantoi, 1999, p. 9).

In Transnistria, the authorities continue the Soviet tradition of emphasizing the multiethnic nature of their society. Thus, street signs are trilingual and the Transnistrian coat-of-arms – clearly an adaptation of the old Soviet coat-of-arms – carries the full name or abbreviation for the self-declared Transnistrian Moldavian Republic in the languages of all three major ethnic groups, placing the Romanian variant in Cyrillic script at the centre (see pictures 2.3 and 2.4). However, the Transnistrian re-

Picture 2.3 Street sign in Tiraspol with "Moldovan", Russian and Ukrainian variants, though the sign above it (only in Russian) shows which language really dominates public life in Transnistria

Picture 2.4 Transnistrian coat of arms in the streets of Tiraspol

gime also continues the Soviet tradition of *de facto* Russian dominance, linguistically and otherwise.

The assertion of Russian linguistic dominance over the large Ukrainian minority is fairly easy, owing to high levels of assimilation (Zaporojan-Pirgari, 2004, p. 65) through generations of Russian and Soviet rule and/or to generally held pro-Russian attitudes in line with many of their ethnic fellows in neighbouring parts of Ukraine. In contrast, the relationship with the Romanian majority is a more complicated one. On the one hand, many urban Romanians have been assimilated and are loyal to the regime. Some even occupy prominent positions in the Transnistrian administration (Troebst, 2003, p. 440). On the other hand, their ethnic ties with the absolute majority of the Chişinău-controlled Bessarabia make them a potential internal enemy in the conflict in the eyes of those who see the conflict in ethnic terms. As the Transnistrian leaders see it in such terms, or at least claim to do so, it is not surprising that they try to reduce the influence of Romanians, whilst also not being too harsh in order to prevent turning this substantial proportion of the population against them.

Amongst other things, the Transnistrian authorities carefully control the linguistic and educational rights of the local Romanians. Whilst in their private lives Transnistrian Romanians are free to use their native language freely, and speaking it publicly does not usually involve any dangers, official use is more restricted. Of the three "state" languages – "Moldovan", Ukrainian and Russian – only the latter is used in the public sphere for official purposes, and Soviet era nationality politics are perpetuated. Thus, in Transnistrian schools Romanian teachers have to use the Cyrillic script, and pupils are still taught that the language is called "Moldovan" and substantially different from Romanian. The few schools that continue to use the Latin script for Romanian and teach according to the Moldovan curriculum have been repeatedly harassed and reduced in numbers on the grounds that they neglected to officially register with the authorities (Hanne, 2004, p. 83).

Of course this is just an excuse, as the registration process is not likely to be made easy for the schools and will not necessarily allow them to continue to operate in their current form after registering and submitting to the controls of the Transnistrian "government". Similarly problematic is the assertion that Cyrillic is the actual native alphabet for "Moldovan". True, enforcing the Cyrillic script is not so much a step backward as it is the prevention of a reform (Hofbauer, 2006). After all, until the 19th century Romanian used to be written in Cyrillic everywhere, making it the odd one out in the family of Romance languages. Nonetheless, at a time when virtually all important Romanian literature and correspondence uses the Latin alphabet and the rest of Moldova has adapted to this change, the retention of Cyrillic in Transnistria is an anachronism, imposed for political reasons, depriving Romanians of their rights to cultural self-determination.

Finally, there are a number of religious divisions to add to the list: In the mass demonstrations leading to Moldova's independence during *perestroika*, amidst general anti-Russian and pro-Romanian slogans the call appeared to send "[t]he Russians over the Dniester, the Jews into the Dniester" (Hofbauer, 2003, p. 132). This was a disturbing echo of the similar slogans heard half a century earlier, when Germans and Romanians brought their projects of mass extermination of the Jews to Ukraine and Moldova, killing on a massive scale and also deporting many Jews to Transnistria (Deletant, 2003; Hausleitner, 2001). However, these slogans did not represent a sudden general revival of the anti-Semitic (and anti-Russian) spirit of the time when Romania ruled Moldova.[5] Although, to some extent, these emotions were building on the general mistrust of Jews that had been cultivated in the Soviet Union and neighbouring Romania, they do not appear to have been felt by too large a proportion of the population. Evidence for this cannot only be found in the fact that luckily no violence against Jews followed these slogans, but also in the view of Jewish organisations that, in contrast to neighbouring countries, today anti-Semitism is not deemed a major issue in Moldova, although there is some evidence of discrimination against Jews in Transnistria (King, 2000, p. 174).

The main religious division in independent Moldova actually lies within the Orthodox Church.[6] Whilst the overwhelming majority of Moldovans, including Romanians, Russians, Ukrainians and even the Turkic speaking Gagauz minority, are orthodox Christians, there is more than one Orthodox Church. The biggest one is the Moldovan Orthodox Church which is affiliated with the Russian Orthodox Church and is treated preferentially by Moldovan state authorities. Its leaders receive diplomatic passports, are invited to official events, and cases of restitution of – or compensation for – property expropriated from them in the Soviet era are facilitated (U.S. Department of State, 2004). The smaller Bessarabian Orthodox Church on the other hand is discriminated against. It has been denied the right to register as a religious community and is thus unable to own property and conduct full-scale religious and

---

[5] However, through such slogans Moldova's minorities were certainly reminded of the time when all of them suffered at the hands of the Romanian regime and thus became more susceptible to separatist ideas.

[6] See interview of the author by "Vatican Radio" (Küchler, 2007b).

community activities, let alone to try to reclaim pre-Communist church property (Dungaciu, 2005b). It claims, nonetheless, that it is the real successor of the Romanian Orthodox Church in Moldova. This is what makes it a thorn in the eye of not just the Moldovan Orthodox Church, but also the state authorities, which see it as too pro-Romanian and thus a threat to Moldovan independence. Would it not see the river Dniester as its boundary by defining itself as a Bessarabian Church, it would surely have great problems in Transnistria, too, as the separatists see Romania as an even bigger threat than Bessarabian Moldova, due to their fear of Romanian-Moldovan (re)unification. For comparison, other small religious communities without such political implications have generally not encountered major problems, although there have been instances of Muslim organisations, Jehovah's Witnesses and even non-believers being harassed by state authorities, orthodox Christians and even priests in both Bessarabia and Transnistria (U.S. Department of State, 2004).

There is therefore a rather long list of issues involving ethnicity, language and religious matters in Moldova, most of which are subjects of ardent debates and political conflict, both within and between the Bessarabian and Transnistrian parts of Moldova. All this seemingly reaffirms the image of an ethnically volatile country. However, Moldova is much less ethnically divided than it may seem, and the Transnistria conflict is not purely an ethnic conflict. In fact, its basis may not be ethnic at all.

From the outset, the great majority of Romanians who participated in the movement towards independence only wanted control over local resources and decision-making, as well as an official recognition of their mother tongue as the language of state and to write that language in the Latin script (Crowther, 1997b, p. 291). It was the extremists of the "Popular Front" who installed themselves at the top of the masses and added the more radical pro-Romanian, anti-Russian and even anti-Semitic elements. Evidence of this is to be found not only in contemporary and current public opinion polls (Katchanovski, 2006), but also in the fact that the radical slogans were not followed by radical deeds. After all, there were no mass killings or other forms of collective violence against Russians or Jews, even though the power vacuum accompanying the collapse of the Soviet Union would have probably allowed for such drastic actions to take place. Moreover, the choice of words of the aforementioned unfortunate slogan is revealing in itself, as it was the Jews, not the Russians – the supposed main enemy in this "ethnic conflict" – who were to be thrown into the Dniester.

Admittedly, the Popular Front did a good job at hi-jacking the popular movements and demonstrations, as the generally moderate democratic opposition was poorly organised (Crowther, 2004b, p. 47). The Front even managed to capture the government bodies of early independent Moldova. However, the speedy loss of support for this grouping, as well its successive splits and moves to more moderate positions are revealing of the actual popular mood (Crowther, 2004b, p. 32; King, 2000, p. 154). In Transnistria, on the other hand, the leadership that led the region into *de facto* independence has been more successful at staying in power. This could be seen as an indication that the Transnistrian public supports its anti-Moldovan and anti-Romanian course and shares its fears of Chişinău's or Bucharest's "imperialism".

It is important, however, not to neglect the stabilising role of presence of the Russian 14th Army which supports the Transnistrian regime with equipment, "volunteers" and general cover for its activities. It allowed the regime to pose as the winner of the Transnistria conflict and consolidate its authoritarian power, thus preventing any more moderate forces from coming to power. In the meantime, strong vested interests in the *status quo* have been created, and a new generation of Transnistrians – more susceptible to twisted tales of ethnicity and imperialism in Transnistria and lacking any sense of affiliation with the Moldovan state – is growing up (Nantoi, 2002, p. 1; Popescu, 2004, p. 13).

Whilst Moldova-proper does appear to need the official domination of ethnic Romanians and the Romanian language in order to sustain its young sovereignty, at the same time it unofficially accepts the *de facto* domination of Russian in many areas to keep the large Slavic minorities content. A similar compromise is reflected in the foreign policy orientation of the country, which – for internal as well as for external reasons – generally tries to strike a balance between a pro-Western and a pro-Russian position or oscillates between the two (Tcaci, 2005, p. 2). Similarly, Transnistria retains its ethnically loaded anti-Romanian and anti-imperialist rhetoric to justify its "independence". Even there, however, the minorities are relatively content. The Transnistrian elites are eager to point out – and to some extent justified in claiming – that Transnistrian Romanians feel different from their ethnic kin in Bessarabia and that many of them support the regime, or at least Transnistrian separatism in general (Ryan, 2006). Some ethnic Romanians – including Moldovan top officers – even chose the side of the Transnistrian separatist forces in the hot phase of the conflict (Malek, 2006, p. 142).

Moreover, in both Bessarabia and Transnistria and between them, ethnically based conflict is virtually absent at the personal level (Malek, 2006, p. 166). Romanians live door-to-door with Russians, intermarriage is common, and there are virtually no instances of ethnic cleansing or ghettoisation of minorities. Whilst conflicts such as the Yugoslav civil war have shown that peoples living peacefully together as neighbours and linked by intermarriage can be mobilised into killing each other based on – imagined or real – ethnic criteria, there are no signs in that direction in Moldova. There is also little religious or linguistic conflict at the personal level. The members of the two conflicting orthodox churches share the same beliefs and religious practices and largely leave the conflict to their political and spiritual leaders (U.S. Department of State, 2004). Admittedly, language politics are a sensitive issue in both parts of Moldova, but anybody is free to use his or her own language in public. The largely bilingual populations of Bessarabia and Transnistria often seem amused or puzzled when foreigners switch from Romanian to Russian and vice-versa when crossing the Dniester.

Crowther (2004b, p. 47) recognises the current absence of ethnic conflict when he states that Moldova differs from other countries in that there the "[...] cycle of ethnic conflict was broken". However, arguably in retrospect there is little evidence that the masses were steering into ethnic conflict in the first place. Rather, it was a subgroup of the elites who picked up the ethnic discourse. In Bessarabia it was the pan-Romanianist Popular Front, whereas in Transnistria it was a group of factory directors, led by current "president" Smirnov proclaiming their opposition to a supposedly imminent "Romanianisation" of Moldova's minorities (Hofbauer, 2006, p. 132). It is of course possible, that the leadership of both conflict parties truly thought that there would be ethnic conflict at the mass level so that each set of elites thought to be selflessly acting in the best interest of the local populations. However, given the generally corrupt and self-interested nature of politicians on both sides and the readiness with which many of them moderated their extremist positions to secure influential posts in government and industry, this scenario seems rather unlikely.

There is, nonetheless, a careful balance in the arrangements between the different ethnicities in Moldova. Therefore, whenever too big changes are suggested, nationalists and those with vested interests in the *status quo* mobilise extremist forces, thus making it look as if there was ethnic conflict. For this reason, the Russian language has not been upgraded to an official language of state, and any solutions involving power-sharing, or otherwise changing the balance of power between Bessarabia and Transnistria or between Romanians and Russians, are fiercely resisted by whatever side feels like it has something to lose – sometimes by both.

In any case, whether ethnic or not, since there was an outbreak of overt conflict with a short hot phase of fighting, its underlying reasons and effects have to be dealt with. A solution is needed in order to bring peace, stability and prosperity to all of Moldova and to stop the negative impacts the *status quo* has on neighbouring countries. It is not needed, however, to prevent a renewed major outbreak of violence, as this is currently rather unlikely:

It is another common misrepresentation to portray the Transnistria conflict as a "frozen conflict", as this gives the image of a fragile and temporary armistice that could break into renewed shooting at any time. In reality, Transnistrian and Moldovan forces patrol the "border" together with Russian military in a joint "peacekeeping force" whilst citizens from both sides, and of all ethnicities, pass back and forth unmolested on a daily basis.[7] Rather, it is the solution that has been frozen, as Dungaciu (2005b, p. 187) rightly points out. This will be highlighted by the later analysis of the history of failed resolution attempts that have left the situation in Transnistria virtually unchanged since the mid-1990s.

Given these fundamental misunderstandings of the situation, it is no surprise that there are also many flawed ideas about possible outcomes and solutions of the conflict. For example, the idea that Moldova could split among ethnic lines and be divided between neighbouring countries (Romania and Ukraine or Russia) as a culmination of – or even a solution to – the conflict is very common in both academic literature[8] and the media. However, this would not only be impossible without creating substantial minorities or carrying out massive ethnic cleansing, due to the heterogeneity of the population in all parts of Moldova, but it would also lack sufficient popular support at least in Bessarabia. As Katchanovski (2006, p. 101) points out, in "[t]he March 1994 referendum [only] 5 percent [of Moldovans] supported the unification of Moldova with Romania", and this was only shortly after the hot phase of the supposedly ethnic conflict.

Both journalists and academics often spread a wrong image about the Transnistria conflict. Whilst they correctly identify many issues involved – including those identified below as impinging on EU interest, they often oversimplify or plainly misrepresent what lies at the basis of the conflict. Parallels to ethnic conflicts in other parts of the former com-

---

[7] The author has even witnessed a Moldovan policeman passing the Transnistrian "border" on a public bus in full uniform, unmolested by the Transnistrian "border officials".

[8] See for example Pirchner (2005)

munist world are readily identified and solutions proposed to be imported.

It is clearly tempting to see the conflict in this way, as it does indeed involve different ethnic groups and some tensions between ethnic majorities and minorities. The author himself almost fell into this trap, when he began researching Moldova, in that he was contemplating theories of nationalism and the social construction of ethnicity in order to understand the basis of the Transnistria conflict. However, it has been shown here that portraying the Transnistria conflict as an essentially ethnic conflict is not just an oversimplification, but plainly wrong.

Nonetheless, the common misrepresentations of the conflict have affected political decision-makers and thus have visible impacts on the positions of the conflicting parties as well as the international actors involved in the conflict resolution process. However, ethnicity is not the only explanation that has been applied to the Transnistria conflict. The following section critically analyses other approaches to the conflict, thus trying to get closer to what really lies at its core and creating a basis for better informed attempts to resolve the conflict.

2.3 Roots of the conflict

Huntington (1997) situates all of Moldova clearly within the Russia-centred orthodox civilisation, making the early years of independence and the Transnistria conflict a short-lived aberration from its otherwise pro-Russian course. However, Moldova has been essentially torn between Moscow and the West throughout its short history of independence. Therefore, Huntington's framework neither explains the Transnistria conflict, nor is it otherwise useful for understanding the realities of Moldova's internal or foreign policy.

In an attempt to build on and improve Huntington's flawed civilisation-based approach and to create something more applicable to Moldova and Ukraine, Katchanovski (2006) argues that the different historical experiences of the different parts of these countries explain the regional variations in political culture and thus the conflict of elites. And indeed, in Moldova history has contributed to the division of elites, or rather the creation of two separate elites in Bessarabia and Transnistria:

As has been mentioned above, Transnistria had been longer under Russian rule and was part of the Soviet Union almost uninterruptedly, whereas Bessarabia enjoyed a year of independence and a lengthy period of Romanian rule in the interwar years and the first years of the Second World War. Therefore, the Transnistrian elites were seen as more reliable when the Moldovan SSR was created in 1940, and this remained the case later on (Spinner, 2003). Also, in Transnistria the Russians – who were the preferred agents of Soviet power – formed a bigger percentage of the population than in Bessarabia. Moreover, they were continuously reinforced in numbers by newly arriving Russians and Ukrainians, who were sent in the framework of Soviet industrialisation projects on the left bank of the Dniester or built holiday and retirement homes in this area not far from the Black Sea, whilst Romanians from all parts of the country were deported or ordered to work in other parts of the Soviet Union in large numbers (International Crisis Group, 2003, p. 2). Therefore, Soviet Moldova's politics were from the outset dominated by Transnistrians. It was for this reason that Bessarabian elites of all ethnicities were more inclined towards the independence movement, whereas the Transnistrian ruling class was anxious to preserve the Soviet Union or at least retain its power (Katchanovski, 2006, p. 101). Eventually it could do so only within its home base to the left of the Dniester.

This does not mean, however, that history dictated all the elements of the game. Moreover, it can be questioned whether the political culture of the two sets of elites in Bessarabia and Transnistria really differs so much. Whilst in the case of Bessarabia there is a comparatively bigger spectrum of political orientations and a larger presence of reform-oriented forces than in Transnistria, arguably the similarities outweigh the differences. In both cases, leaders have generally tended to come from the former communist organisations and to different extents even continued to embrace many of the old communist values and symbols. Even though ideological differences may have played a role in the beginning of the conflict (Pop, 2003), it is not immediately apparent why the more industrial Transnistrian elites and the more agrarian Bessarabian elites should not have found a way of sharing power by concentrating on their respective sectors.

Today, in both parts of Moldova, corruption is a way of life, and all branches of government as well as the media are frequently used by those who manage to capture them for political and private ends (International Crisis Group, 2003, p. 28; Clej & Canţîr, 2004). Moreover, there are historical and current links between organisations and individuals from the two sides. Like many influential Moldovans, president Voronin was actually born in Transnistria. Whilst he has cut most of the links to his birthplace and is no longer welcome there,[9] others have not. Business-people from both sides trade with the supposed enemy, or in other ways benefit from the *status quo*.[10] Both the creation of the conflict and the freezing of its solution have served particular elites' interests. The longer the solution to the conflict has been dragged out, the more firmly those elites with vested interests have reinforced their positions. In the meantime many others have accommodated themselves to the situation, seeing how they, too, can profit from the *status quo*.

One could of course attempt to portray the Transnistria conflict as an essentially regionalist one (Hanne, 1998, p. 7), as both conflicting parties are based in clearly defined regions and regionalism often results from local elites' separate interests. Such conflicts of interests can become violent, leading to civil wars at the most extreme end of the spec-

---

[9] Although Voronin's mother continued to live in Transnistria, he only came there for her funeral, according to Iryna Severyn, a former advisor of his who was interviewed by the author in Kyiv in March 2007.

[10] Author's interview with Rosaria Puglisi, Senior Advisor to the EU Special Representative to Moldova in Kyiv on 08/12/2006.

trum of regionalism. Regional elites may even attempt to construct a separate national identity to justify more extreme stances including separatist secession. To some extent, this is happening in Transnistria, where the leadership is desperately trying to carve out a separate Transnistrian historical and cultural identity for its population as a whole, through twisting facts and appropriating historical figures with little connection to this strip of land.[11] However, taking a closer look, the issue is not that the dominant Slavic minorities are claiming that they are any different from Bessarabian Russians and Ukrainians, but rather that the Russian elites attempt to carve out a separate Transnistrian Moldovan identity for the Romanian plurality. Such an imposed regionalism, affecting only a part of the population and originating neither from within that part of the public, nor its own elites, is barely regionalism at all.

Picture 2.5 Honorary citizens of Tiraspol: Mostly Russians – from Russia

---

[11] Historical figures who appear on Transnistrian banknotes, as statues in its parks, or are in other ways publicly honoured in Transnistria often have little connection to the region. They are, however, generally ethnic Russians or Ukrainians, in contrast to Bessarabia, which shares its most important "national" heroes with Romania.

Therefore, it can be said that neither Huntington's cultural determinism and clash of civilisations, nor Katchanovski's historical determinism and clash of political culture, nor the concept of regionalism fully explain the conflict between the Bessarabian and Transnistrian elites and thus the Transnistria conflict. In fact, it is more convincing to see these two elites merely as competing "clans" of similarly minded elites, each defending their economic interests[12] and the populations of both sides as simply caught up in this situation and not substantially different from their counterparts on the other side of the Dniester.

As neighbouring Ukraine has shown, populations can eventually turn against vested interests. Thus, the relative absence of movements for a kind of "Orange Revolution" in both parts of Moldova points to the existence of other factors. At first sight it may appear as though the Transnistrian leadership simply averted such a movement by its authoritarian course, together with a clever mobilisation of young people through such pro-regime movements as the youth organisation *Proriv* (Hofbauer, 2006).[13] In contrast, the leaders of Moldova-proper – particularly president Voronin – seemed for some time to have "turned orange" themselves, by drastically reversing their course (Dungaciu, 2005b; Oertel, 2005). Taking a closer look, however, one realises that the leaders of both parts of Moldova are very responsive to – and dependent on – external forces, rather than internal movements.

Owing to its small size and weak economy, Moldova is much more vulnerable than its big neighbour Ukraine. Therefore, in the current absence of a substantive European perspective, it remains heavily dependent on the Russian Federation (Spanu, 2004). Russia, however, is everything but a benevolent protector of Moldovan interests. It uses its economic and military presence in the country to further its own economic and geo-political interests in the region and does not hesitate to let Moldova know when its policies are not well received in Moscow. A good example of such behaviour is Russia's recent blockade of Moldovan

---

[12] Author's interview with Rosaria Puglisi, 08/12/2006.
[13] See pictures 2.6 and 2.7

THE EU IN MOLDOVA'S TRANSNISTRIA CONFLICT 53

Picture 2.6 Transnistrian interpretation of "civil society": Headquaters of the pro-separatist and pro-Russian youth movement *Proriv* (logo flags enlarged) in Tiraspol

Picture 2.7 The source of *Proriv's* inspiration: Flags of the Ukrainian *Pora* movement, part of the anti-Russian "Orange Revolution" movement. Apart from the yellow flags with black diagonal writing, however, the two organisations have little in common.

wine, officially due to "quality" issues, but generally accepted to be a politically motivated punishment for Moldova's recent reorientation towards the West and its "blockade" of Transnistria.[14]

Picture 2.8 Business as usual: The DHL office in Tiraspol

Whilst Transnistria has been lucky in that it contains most of Moldova's industry and electricity generation capacity, it too is dependent on Russia. Its whole financial and energy sectors are controlled by Russian companies, and Russian investors play the biggest role in the illegal privatisation of Moldovan state enterprises located in Transnistria (Burla, 2005, p. 21). Russian funds and energy deliveries keep the regime afloat, especially in times of crises. This is symbolised by the fact that the

---

[14] The Moldovan government has been accused by the Transnistrians of an economic blockade against their "nation". In reality, Moldova simply made arrangements with Ukraine, ensuring that only those goods on which tax has been paid to the Moldovan government would pass the border. The Transnistrians could have easily paid this minimal tax, but instead chose to shut down much of their cross-border trade with Ukraine, thus effectively blockading themselves (International Crisis Group, 2006, p. 8).

local branch of the Russian "Gazprombank" is headquartered in one of Tiraspol's most modern buildings and even features on the cities' official postcards. Whilst there are also Western companies operating in – and trading with – Transnistria (see picture 2.8), these are nowhere near as numerous and as vital to Transnistria as their Russian counterparts.

Russia has the power, though currently not the will, to put an end to the Transnistria conflict by withdrawing its one-sided support. However, Russia – or at least certain Russian circles – chose to support the separatists from the outset. The Russian 14th Army lent its unofficial support in the form of equipment and "volunteers" to the Transnistrians in the hot phase of the war. Whilst it is disputed whether the Russian government had ordered these measures, or whether General Lebed of the 14th Army was acting on his own (Fodor, 1995, p. 170), this was far from being the only Russian support to the regime. Other volunteers, including battle-hungry Cossacks, came all the way from Russia to fight on the side of the separatists (Ascherson, 1996, p. 102). As soon as the hot phase of the war was over, Russia used various forms of soft power and citizenship policies, turning Transnistria into an almost *de facto* Russian region and many Transnistrians into Russian citizens (Pirchner, 2005). Moreover, the legal foundation has been created to make Transnistrian official accession to the Russian Federation possible, and Russian officials have repeatedly called for the application of the Montenegro or Kosovo precedent to Transnistria, allowing it to become independent as an intermediary step to becoming part of Russia (Pirchner, 2005).

The Transnistrian regime is thus but a puppet and Moldova as a whole a rather powerless subject of Russian geo-political and economic interests. Whilst it sometimes may seem unclear as to who is holding the strings in Moscow, as the Russian government tends to officially distance itself from the Transnistrian regime, this is likely to be a deliberate deception in order to claim the role of the neutral arbitrator and justify the continued Russian military presence in Moldova. Russian claims that the tiny PMR is preventing the withdrawal of the remainder of the 14th Army, or in any other ways has power over Moscow, are rather absurd (Malek, 2006,

p. 168; Sysoyev, 2007). True, Transnistria has developed dynamics of its own, but the Russians have the power to put an end to any unwelcome developments there immediately by simply withdrawing their substantial support.

Moldova is relatively small and unimportant, so that it may not be immediately clear what Russia gains from its control over the country. However, Moldova lies at the doorstep of NATO and the European Union and is also close to the Black Sea. It is therefore of strategic importance for Russian companies and military planners alike. Russian energy corporations and trading companies see Moldova as an actual or potential transit land for energy deliveries to – and trade with – the EU and the Balkans, whereas the Russian military sees it as an outpost against the continuously enlarging NATO (Malek, 2006, p. 168). Given that NATO "moved into" several formerly Russian-dominated countries and even post-Soviet states as soon as Russia lost its position of military and economic domination, and given the recent troubles in Russian-Ukrainian and Russian-Belarusian relations, Transnistria can even be framed as the last Russian stronghold in the Western CIS.

The Russian presence in Transnistria is the westernmost location of Russian troops in South-Eastern Europe and would be the only outpost on non-Russian soil in the Black Sea area when the agreement on Russia's use of the Ukrainian port of Sevastopol runs out in 2017, unless Russia succeeds in negotiating an extension to this arrangement. General Lebed even went as far as calling Moldova "the key to the Balkans" that is vital to Russian influence in the region (Waters, 2003, p. 193). All this gives Russia a great incentive for either delaying the resolution of the Transnistria conflict or pressing for those solutions that ensure Russia's continued military and economic presence in Moldova. Moreover, any country under Russia's tutelage provides additional votes for Russia – or at least abstentions – in international organisations.

In conclusion it can be said that whilst history and geography prepared the playing field, it was the clashes of similar, but rivalling, local elites and contemporary geopolitics which created the rules of the game and continue to prevent a resolution of the conflict. In essence the Transnistria conflict is not an internal ethnic conflict, but an international one between Moldova and Russia, although the latter often uses the Transnistrians as a proxy. Moldovan politics is thus best understood as the desperate attempt to maintain a distance from both Romania and Russia, whilst being culturally dependent on the former and economically on the latter. Transnistrian politics, by contrast, are merely a projection of Russian interests in the country and region. This needs to be taken into account by any proposed solution to the conflict. The next chapter shows that this has not always been the case.

3 International conflict resolution efforts

In the 15 years since the 1992 hot phase of the Transnistria conflict, the format of international conflict resolution has changed many times, but so far nothing substantial has been achieved, despite the signing of around 50 common declarations by the conflicting sides and several resolutions by international organisations (Malek, 2006, p. 159). This section analyses the most important episodes, concepts and actors involved in the conflict resolution attempts to date in order to inform the analysis which follows. Table 3.1 summarises the key events related to conflict resolution efforts.

3.1 History

International efforts to solve the Transnistria conflict began even before its actual hot phase. Following the Transnistrian declaration of independence, a whole wave of discussions and declarations in support of Moldova swept through international organisations. Concrete attempts to find a solution were, however, left to individual groups of states. The first set of states attempting to find a solution consisted of Moldova and the "external guarantors" Russia, Romania and Ukraine (Pop, 2003, p. 210). However, Moldova itself was divided by the conflict, and Russia was a *de facto* participant on the side of the separatists. Thus, the conflict was in essence an international one between Moldova and Russia, and the latter was in no position to play the role of a neutral arbitrator for a peaceful solution and external guarantor for the former's sovereignty and territorial integrity. Moreover, both Romania and Ukraine had actual or potential interests in parts or all of Moldova and to different extents also became involved in the fighting.[15] Therefore, the format was less than ideal from the outset due to the lack of neutral arbitrators and the severe bias of the most powerful country involved. The outcomes of this quadrilateral negotiation – during its short life – thus heavily favoured the Transnistrian/Russian side.

Table 3.1 Key events in the international search for a solution

Date	Event
20 March 1992	CIS declaration stressing Moldova's territorial integrity
6 April 1992	Moldova, Russia, Romania and Ukraine set up a quadripartite commission to implement a ceasefire and disengagement
25 June 1992	Joint communiqué of the four states at the BSEC summit calling for an immediate ceasefire and disengagement
3 July 1992	Meeting between Russian and Moldovan presidents
21 July 1992	Ceasefire agreement signed between Russia (!) and Moldova; Tripartite Commission of Control created by Russia, Moldova and Transnistria
April 1993	Permanent CSCE mission to Moldova commences its work
28 April 1994	Parcani agreements commence status negotiations between Moldova and Transnistria
July 1994	Moldovan parliament approves Transnistrian autonomy
21 October 1994	Moldovan and Russian prime ministers agree 3-year schedule for Russian military withdrawal

---

[15] Romania sent some material and logistical supply to the Moldovan government (Ozhiganov, 1997, p. 178) whereas Ukrainian nationalists – normally fiercely anti-Russian – supported the Transnistrian separatists (United Press International, 2007) to save their ethnic kin and the other Slavs of the region from the feared "Romanianisation" (Hofbauer, 2006, p. 132). Their convictions that they were fighting Romanian imperialism were naturally reinforced by Romania's actions. However, the extent of Romanian involvement in the conflict has often been vastly exaggerated.

February 1995	OSCE mission branch office opened in Tiraspol
Summer 1995	Russian 14th Army renamed "Operational Group of Forces in Moldova"
4 September 1995	Transnistria celebrates "Independence Day"
March 1997	OSCE Ambassador declared *persona non grata* in Transnistria
8 May 1997	Moscow Memorandum (Primakov Memorandum) on the normalisation of relations signed by Moldova and Transnistria and international guarantors (Russia, Ukraine, OSCE)
23 December 1997	Agreement on Russian withdrawal of military equipment
5 February 1998	The PMR declares its statehood
20 March 1998	Odesa agreement on confidence building measures and development of contact between Moldova and Transnistria
March 1999	Russian Duma declares Transnistria an area of strategic interest
November 1999	OSCE Istanbul summit agreement on Russian withdrawal by 2002
19 May 2001	Russian-Moldovan friendship treaty, naming Russia the guarantor of Moldova's territorial integrity
November 2003	Kozak Memorandum foreseeing the federalisation of Moldova
13 February 2004	OSCE plan for federalising Moldova

(Fodor, 1995; Malek, 2006; OSCE, 1997/1998/1999; Severin, 2004)

The format that replaced this quadrilateral setup was by no means better. By the time of the ceasefire agreement, quadrilateral conflict resolution had been reduced to an ostensibly trilateral setting (Pop, 2003, p. 210), although actually two countries – Romania and Ukraine – were removed from the process. This was due to the fact that, from then onwards, Transnistria was counted separately from both Moldova and Russia, despite the fact that it was legally part of the former and effectively formed a common conflict party with the latter. This reflected Russia's successful dual strategy of awarding Transnistria the position of a *de facto* independent actor on the international stage with essentially the same weight as Moldova proper, whilst also keeping an official distance from its client "state" in order to retain the pose of a neutral arbitrator.

Slowly, however, other actors were also admitted to the process. The first and most important actor to join the conflict resolution effort officially was the Organisation for Security and Cooperation in Europe (OSCE), which was still the Conference on Security and Cooperation in Europe (CSCE) when it became involved in 1993. It joined the trilateral group, first as an observer, then as a full participant, whilst itself increasingly turning into a forum for more multilateral conflict resolution efforts with a particular focus on reaching agreement on a Russian military withdrawal from Transnistria (Pop, 2003, p. 210; Severin, 2004, p. 162).

Along with the OSCE, Ukraine also rejoined the process, making the process more inclusive by bringing the number of actors involved to five – if counted the in way that Russia does it. However, this did not result in more balanced outcomes and is even referred to by some as a "four-versus-one" approach, implying that Russia frequently manages to get all actors lined up against Moldovan interests (Socor, 2005b). It is also notable that Romania never returned to the core group of negotiators. This was partially due to a lack of initiative on Romania's part and partially to Russian reservations (Dungaciu, 2005b).

Finally, in 2005 the EU and the United States joined the negotiating framework, but only as observers. For this reason, the current negotiating format is referred to as "five-plus-two". Despite the fact that Moldova had temporarily withdrawn from negotiations in 2004 as an act of protest against the lack of participation of the EU and the US, "the two" seem to be content with their rather limited status, and the format remains the same (Socor, 2005b).

3.2 Actors

Transnistria was the first actor in the conflict, as everything started with its declaration of independence. Ever since Russia rushed to its aid, however, the PMR has retained little of its own agency. It has thus generally behaved like a tame puppet (Nantoi, 2005b, p. 4) in the conflict resolution process, being more conciliatory when this was in Russia's interest, or retreating to hard-line positions when Russia loosened its strings. Russian efforts to portray the Transnistrians as independent actors and Moscow's policies as merely reacting to the separatists' actions, are easily exposed as propaganda, given the extent of Russian support discussed above.

Nonetheless, it is conceivable that Transnistria – whether under its current leadership or not – could regain its agency if its interests begin to significantly diverge from those of Moscow. This new agency could be applied in a proactive or reactive way, depending on the scenario. For example, Transnistria could decide that it has an interest in solving the crisis and reuniting with Moldova, or it could act on its own after being abandoned by Russia. In the latter case both a renewed escalation and a swift solution to the conflict would be possible.

Moldova itself has been a very weak and unassertive actor in the conflict with the breakaway region. In fact, Russia has exercised almost equal amounts of control over both parts of Moldova, despite only having troops in Transnistria and Bessarabian part of the so-called "security zone" – a thin strip of land along the Dniester[16]. Although Chişinău never gave in to the most radical demands no matter what the pressure, it has

---

[16] See map on page 25.

been highly conciliatory with Russia and Transnistria most of the time. Slightly more assertive stances, including the last-minute dropout from the 2003 Russian-sponsored federalisation imitative, were usually coinciding with a more Western reorientation of the country and the involvement of the West in Moldova (Hofbauer, 2006).

Notably, the period of the most recent pro-Western turn that lasted from late 2003 to 2006 saw the country led by the Communist Party of Moldova, which had won a majority of votes in 2001 on a pro-Russian ticket. If even these forces attempted to break with Russia, it must have seemed to many as though Moldova was all set to escape from the Russian domination. Recently, however, Moldova has reverted to the humiliating approach of 2001, naming Russia the guarantor of Moldovan integrity, despite all evidence to the contrary (Malek, 2006, p. 160). This was due to the lack of genuine support from the West, coupled with severe Russian pressure in the form of economic embargoes and a loosening of Transnistria's strings. This renewed change of attitudes in turn has lost Moldovan president Voronin goodwill in the West, whilst Russia is only reluctantly phasing out its most severe pressures. Thus, Moldova's switching back and forth has done more damage than it has yielded benefits, leaving the country in an even weaker position. From such a weak position, it would be even harder to assert Moldovan interests if its leadership were to be forced to choose sides permanently between Russia and the EU. The country is simply not strong enough and also not important enough – at least to the West – to be able to exploit its position between two camps. After all, the Cold War is over, despite the fact that the situation in Moldova is a relic from this time and Transnistria resembles the late Soviet Union in many aspects (Brezianu & Spânu, 2007). Therefore, everything depends on the actions of more powerful outside actors.

The key actor is, of course, Russia which – whilst it controls the two conflict parties to great extents and is a *de facto* party to the conflict – also poses as the principal "peacekeeper" and key participant in the conflict resolution process. Throughout the history of conflict resolution attempts Russia has ensured its ownership of the process and ignored or reinterpreted international agreements and resolutions, regardless of whether it had signed them (Malek, 2006, p. 151). Moscow has, however, continued with its masquerade of presenting crude bullying and sphere of influence politics as if they were the actions of a responsible and benevolent regional power. This began with the construction of a threat to Transnistria ostensibly posed by the Moldovan government and Romania, thus enabling Russia to justify its intervention on "humanitarian grounds" and in the name of "self-determination" of the Transnistrian "nation". At the same time, the official non-recognition by Russia of its own creation – the PMR[17] – served the dual ends of keeping the strings in Moscow's hands[18] and enabling it to pose as obedient to international law. Russia even sought an official mandate from the United Nations (UN) for its "peacekeeping" mission and – when rejected on the grounds that peacekeeping missions made up from the conflicting parties were against UN principles – began to claim that its method of peacekeeping was superior to that of the UN (Gribincea, 2001, p. 198).

Whilst the conflict resolution process has been dragged out through their consistent vetoes of any proposed solution, Russia and its Transnistrian puppet regime created realities on the ground which further strengthened their negotiating positions. The Transnistrian regime consolidated its power, silenced opposition, built parallel national institutions, replacing those of Moldova and even printed its own money – the Transnistrian Rouble – thus becoming an independent state in all but name and making a future reintegration into Moldova more complicated (Hanne, 2004, p. 81). Meanwhile, Russia gave out passports to a substantial proportion of the Transnistrian population and ensured that the Transnistrian administration approximated to Russian standards and

---

[17] Although Russia entertains quasi-diplomatic relations with Transnistria, it has never gone as far as officially recognising the PMR, which remains "recognised" only by other non-recognised separatist entities.

[18] After all, Moscow does not see value in Transnistrian statehood and agency per se, but rather aims at incorporating it into the Russian federation (Pirchner, 2005).

procedures. Therefore, Russia is increasingly able to frame its military presence in terms of protection of its own citizens abroad and has also prepared the ground for the eventuality of Transnistria's accession to the Russian Federation (Pirchner, 2005).

Nonetheless, when the issue of the its military presence in Moldova came up, Russia often showed a surprising willingness to compromise and even committed itself to complete withdrawal of its troops on several occasions. Whenever the relevant deadlines approached, however, substantial withdrawals were declined or postponed indefinitely with reference to the continued need for Russia's "peacekeeping" role (Gribincea, 2001), thus exposing its commitments as time-buying tactics to create favourable conditions on the ground to prolong the *status quo*. Although partial withdrawals of military equipment and a downsizing of military manpower have occurred, the former has been minute compared to the overall military stocks (Freedomhouse, 2004) in Transnistria and the latter has been offset by the passage of many former Russian soldiers into the Transnistrian army. Moreover, many in the officer-heavy Russian forces in Transnistria either grew up there or grew strong roots through marrying locals and acquiring property and thus would not think about leaving (King, 2000, p. 201). The current official line in Moscow is that its withdrawal from Moldova will only happen in conjunction with the resolution of the Transnistria conflict itself, although such conditions were not included in the various agreements on withdrawal and thus represent unilateral reinterpretations (Severin, 2004, p. 161).

When it comes to conflict resolution attempts itself, however, Moscow holds all the strings in its hands. Thus, Russia either makes proposals that are strongly in its own interest, or maps the said reinterpretation strategies onto agreements already reached, or – as a last resort – simply boycotts the negotiations. These strategies, coupled with the "peacekeeping" argument, ensure that Russia grants itself the license to remain in the area indefinitely. Moldova, starting from a weak bargaining position, has no choice but to acquiesce and has thus at several times even been persuaded to endorse the "peacekeeping" quality of the Russian military presence on its soil (Azi, 2005).

Moreover, in the more recent negotiations and conflict resolution plans, Russia has been very open about its medium to long-term intentions, calling for a prolonged presence of its military bases right from the outset, rather than unilaterally slipping in such demands after agreements have already been reached. However, Russia also increasingly sends signals that – despite its considerable interests in the area – Transnistria is a trump card that can be tossed away when necessary in order to reach other goals (Sysoyev, 2007). Also, there is an increasing realisation in Moscow that the *zadira* or bullying politics applied so far in its near abroad have been counterproductive.[19] Therefore, Russia could potentially become, if not a responsible player, at least a partner with whom one can bargain and reason in order to resolve the Transnistria conflict if one has the right things to offer in return.

Ukraine was part of the international conflict resolution process from the outset. This is not surprising if one considers that the Transnistrians gained control of a significant proportion of the Moldovan-Ukrainian border area and that thus events in the separatist areas impacted on neighbouring Ukrainian areas. Moreover, in the Crimean peninsula Ukraine has a potentially parallel case of pro-Russian separatism. Yet the country allowed itself to be sidelined by Russia relatively quickly and did not take an assertive stance on the issue until in 2005 the pro-Western president Yushchenko presented the conflict resolution plan that carried his name. Even this plan was vague and rather close to the Russian position and had actually been cleared with Moscow in advance (Socor, 2005a).

This – and the preceding reluctance to get involved – can be explained by two factors. Firstly, Ukraine itself has a problematic relationship with Russia and has been essentially divided between pro-Western and pro-Russian forces ever since its independence from the Soviet Un-

---

[19] Author's interview with former EU ambassador to Russia and senior scholar Michael Emerson on 24/03/07 in Kyiv, Ukraine.

ion. Secondly, certain sympathies for – and trade with – the Transnistrians have created a considerable degree of vested interest in the Transnistrian *status quo* in neighbouring regions of Ukraine and even the nation as a whole.[20] As the internal divisions of Ukraine have come to the fore again in 2007, it is questionable whether one should expect a substantial contribution from Ukraine in the near future. However, the mere presence of this relatively benevolent and pro-Western country as a buffer between Moldova and Russia has served as a guarantee of Moldova's independence and prevented a renewed escalation of the Transnistria conflict (Khotin, 2004, p. 144). This passive contribution on the part of Ukraine will continue in the future, unless its government switches to an unquestioning pro-Russian line, which is unlikely even if the more pro-Russian forces – Party of Regions, Communists and Socialists – return to power (see picture 3.1). Their return would, however, be likely to reverse the tightening of the border controls Yushchenko introduced on the Moldovan-Ukrainian border, if not in response to Russian and Transnistrian complaints about "economic blockade", at least for reasons of the economic interests which these parties' elites have in trade with Transnistria (Soros Foundation-Moldova, 2005). For the same reasons, Ukraine – under any government – could not be relied upon for drastic enforcement measures such as cutting off Russian energy supplies to Transnistria if they were to be considered by the West.

Romania, too, has been part of the conflict resolution process from the beginning, naturally on the Moldovan side, which it had also supported to some extent during the fighting. However, this support was clearly linked with Romania's own interests in Moldova. Hence, when it became clearer that Moldova rejected reunification with Romania, the relationship between the two states became a lot more strained and complicated (Serebrian, 2004). Ever since, Romania has had a rather destabilising role, with its irredentist rhetoric leading to quarrels with Chişinău thus alienating the Moldovan side whilst giving the Transnistri-

---

[20] See author's conference paper on Ukrainian interests in the Transnistria conflict (Küchler, 2007c)

Picture 3.1 Supporters of the pro-Russian Party of Regions, Communists and Socialists in Kyiv during the 2007 power struggle which was marginally won by the pro-Western forces of the former orange coalition

ans more opportunities to play on fears of Romanian imperialism. Nonetheless, besides such rhetoric, Romania was pre-occupied with its own Euro-Atlantic integration and thus lacked a clear Moldova strategy (Dungaciu, 2005b, p. 49). In 2005, however, the Romanian president Băsescu called for Romanian, US and EU participation in the conflict resolution process (Malek, 2006, p. 155). As soon as Romania fully overcomes its own recent internal power struggles and fully settles in within the EU, it may become a force to be reckoned with in neighbouring Moldova and the general Black Sea area. Whether it will become engaged in a constructive way, or escalate its Greater Romanian irredentist populism, however, remains to be seen.

Despite declarations in support of the Moldovan government (Cojocaru, 2001, pp. 194-197; U.S. Department of State, 2005) and the negotiation lines of Western actors and the OSCE, the United States has not been directly involved in the resolution attempts for the Transnistria conflict. Nonetheless, the US has had an indirect impact through its membership in the OSCE – whose Moldova mission is headed by an American – and diplomatic manoeuvring at key moments in the negotiation process. Its most direct impact was felt when the US ambassador in Chişinău played a key part in persuading the Moldovan president Voronin to reject the flawed Russian federalisation plan for Moldova based on the Kozak Memorandum at the last minute (Hofbauer, 2003, p. 147). This has not, however, been followed by a constructive engagement and genuine search for an alternative solution. The US has been tied up further east in the last few years. The future of America's involvement in Russia's near abroad will depend on its willingness and ability to have a global involvement in the post-Iraq world. In any case, Washington may no longer be willing to solve Europe's security problems, particularly if it is not directly affected by them.

Several other countries have taken initiatives to resolve the Transnistria conflict. Generally, however, these have tended to coincide with their presidencies or chairmanships of international organisations involved in the process and seldom survived the end of the terms. Bulgaria for example presided over – and pushed forward – the 2004 OSCE plan for the resolution of the Transnistria conflict and the creation of a federal Moldovan state. Also, Moldova and Transnistria are mentioned in several wider regional initiatives by both international organisations and individual states.[21]

The format in which the states took part in the conflict resolution process varied over time, and many countries have been present in several different configurations. At the bilateral level, there were negotiations between Moldova and Transnistria, but more often than not between Moldova and Russia, leaving no doubt as to who was holding the strings in Transnistria (Fodor, 1995). Trilateral settings usually included the two conflicting parties plus Russia, thus essentially representing an asymmetric bilateral setup of Moldova vs. Russia and Transnistria. In the quadrilateral and multilateral settings, they were joined by other states, although Russia remained the dominant power. This is not surprising, considering that Russia is the only power with a clear ability to make or break solutions on the matter.

Increasingly, international organisations have also become involved in the process. At times they represented additional partners in the multilateral negotiations, at other times they simply provided a forum in which national actors could negotiate.

The first international organisation to become active on the Transnistria issue was the CIS. It issued a resolution in support of Moldovan sovereignty and territorial integrity, in line with its charter article 3 on the inviolability of existing CIS borders (Fowler, 1991; Pop, 2003, p. 210). Due to the Russian dominance in this organisation, however, this was rendered meaningless by the further course of events.

Within the CIS, a subgroup of states called GU(U)AM was formed by four states – Georgia, Ukraine, Azerbaijan and Moldova – who had problems with pro-Russian separatists and/or a generally uneasy relationship with Russia, in order to create a counterbalance to Russian dominance. For some time these were also joined by Uzbekistan, hence

---

[21] For examples of EU and EU member states' initiatives, see chapter 4.

the second "U". Their ideas range from parallel pipelines and trade agreements, to alleviate the vulnerability to Russian economic pressure, right into the military sphere through joint exercises and plans for joint peacekeeping contingents for their respective conflicts (GUUAM, 2000; Neukirch, 2004, pp. 137-138). Russia, however, is currently powerful enough to sabotage the first set of plans and would not even consider granting GU(U)AM a role in peacekeeping or even negotiate with the whole group at once.

Similarly, the non-recognised separatist entities have organised their own groupings and meetings. However, due to their non-recognition by the international community and due to the fact that these entities embody the problem, rather than offering a solution, they have not been included in the international conflict resolution process on a collective basis. In any case, there are substantial differences between Transnistria and the other "frozen conflicts" - Abkhazia, South Ossetia and Nagorno Karabakh – so that the international community is well advised to treat them separately and differentially and not negotiate with all of them at once (Boonstra, 2005, p. 7).

The Organisation of Black Sea Economic Cooperation (BSEC) also served as a forum for the discussion of the conflict, and a resolution in support of Moldova was issued there very early during the conflict (Pop, 2003, p. 210). However, the lack of institutional substance – compared to the EU and even the OSCE – has meant that the BSEC has not become an actor on the conflict in its own right. Whether this organisation will have an impact, will to a large extent depend on the extent to which the EU makes use of – and builds on – its recently gained observer status therein, having previously largely ignored it (Emerson et al., 2007a).

Besides the two conflicting parties and Russia, the OSCE has the most constant track record of participation in the various conflict resolution attempts. Unfortunately, this record is a rather negative one, consisting of a long list of failed attempts (Severin, 2004). This is not to say, that the OSCE deserves all of the blame for not solving the conflict. After all it also essentially lacks enforcement mechanisms, so that, as an OSCE member, Russia has been able to consistently sabotage the organisation's efforts by not complying with its resolutions (Severin, 2004, p. 166).

Some would, however, say that the work of the organisation has even been counterproductive, as it has uncritically taken up Russian leads in terms of federalisation solutions for Moldova[22] and accepting Transnistria as a state-like partner in the negotiation process (Malek, 2006, p. 157). In any case, the organisation has become the focus of antipathy from all sides. Transnistria portrays it as an American imperialist instrument, despite the fact that it was created in part through a Soviet initiative to promote détente in the early 1970's. Whilst the current head of the OSCE in Moldova is indeed an American, it is actually the general policy of democratisation and non-recognition of Transnistrian elections that triggers this hatred and leads Transnistrian youth to burn OSCE flags along with Moldovan symbols.[23] At the same time, the organisation as well as its local mission are being accused by Romanians of being not only toothless, but also pro-Russian (Dungaciu, 2005b). The former EU Ambassador to Russia (and now academic observer) Michael Emerson goes so far as to call the OSCE a non-actor, or dead actor, in terms of the Transnistria conflict.[24] Nonetheless, it still chairs meetings in the current negotiating format.

The Transnistria conflict – as well as the general situation in Moldova – has also been discussed at various times in the Parliamentary Assembly of the Council of Europe (PACE) in the framework of its monitoring of the country, most recently in February 2007. A few months before, Council of Europe (CoE) Secretary General Davis expressed his support for the Moldovan government position in the Transnistria issue and offered help whenever it might be needed (BASA-Press, 2006). Despite these words it is unclear how this body could be expected to make a significant contribution where the OSCE has failed, considering its total

---

[22] See chapter 3
[23] This was proudly boasted as a successful political action by representatives of the pro-Separatist youth group *Proriv* to a group of German students with whom the author met in Tiraspol in September 2006.
[24] Interview with the author, 24/03/2007.

lack of enforcement mechanisms, apart from the actual suspension of membership (PACE, 2007). Moreover, its membership is probably too wide and includes too many diverging interests to become seriously active on the issue. Nonetheless, for a conflict that attracts as little attention as the Transnistria conflict, mere deliberation on the issues involved in an international organisations is a positive signal, as it enables other actors – such as the EU – to take up the conclusions reached or follow up the discussions. The most significant conclusion that can be taken up by other actors is that of the CoE's European Court of Human Rights (ECHR) in assigning official responsibility for the Transnistria conflict and thus legal responsibility for its consequences to Russia (Gheorghiu, 2005b, p. 4).

Instead of joining a military CIS alliance, Moldova signed the "Partnership for Peace" document with NATO (Skvortova, 2003, p. 2) in 1994 and – despite their initial protests – even secured the Transnistrians' participation in this framework. Also, like in other CIS states with separatist problems, some in Moldova turned to NATO for a solution, only to be rebuffed and referred to the OSCE instead (Chifu, 2004, p. 89; Malek, 2006, p. 156). Therefore, NATO does not currently have a role in the international conflict resolution process. Moreover, since Moldova insists on its neutrality and strives to stay out of any military security arrangements, a greater role for NATO is not likely to emerge in the near future (Vahl & Emerson, 2004, p. 24). This is actually good news for the conflict resolution process, as the ability of the debate on NATO accession to polarize pro-Western and pro-Russian forces can be witnessed in Ukraine at the moment. Such a polarisation would not be conductive to finding common ground between the Moldovan and Transnistrian leadership and pose a strong incentive for Russia not to withdraw its troops.

As has been stated above, the UN has refused to approve the Russian-led "peacekeeping" mission on the Moldovan-Transnistrian "border". Other than that, few actions were taken by this organisation despite Moldovan appeals, since it was engaged in other parts of the world and could also point to regional organisations which were already involved in the conflict resolution process in Moldova. However, the United Nations Development Programme (UNDP) participates as an implementing partner in the EU Border Assistance Mission (EUBAM) on the Moldovan-Ukrainian border, which will be discussed below (EUBAM, 2006).

Other organisations involved in the conflict's resolution on a minor scale have included the International Red Cross during the hot phase of the conflict (Pop, 2003, p. 211) and numerous democracy and human rights related nongovernmental organisations (NGOs) in its aftermath. The actions of the latter are, however, severely restricted in Transnistria, which allows no foreign funded civil society organisations – including Moldovan ones – to open branches on its soil (International Crisis Group, 2004/2006) and also hinders the operations of visiting organisations.[25]

As a general pattern, the conflict resolution attempts have continuously switched between the international dimension – involving other states and international organisations to balance Russia – and bilateral ones between Moldova and Russia, reflecting the tension between Moldova's aspirations and geopolitical realities.

3.3 Themes and solutions

It has already been argued above, that the dismemberment of Moldova as a country is not a viable option and that its complete disappearance is unlikely. Also, it has been shown that this does not prevent continuing speculations in these directions and – on the part of Russia – actual preparations for such eventualities. There are, however, alternatives which are widely discussed within concerned circles, aimed to pro-

---

[25] The author has gained first-hand experience of this situation when trying – and failing – to organise an election observation mission to Transnistria with an international student organisation for the 2006 referendum on independence from Moldova and accession to the Russian Federation held by the separatists.

vide a true solution to the conflict rather than simply terminating it by keeping the two sides apart once and for all. The two most widely discussed concepts are those of federalisation and democratisation. These are certainly not mutually exclusive.

The federalisation of Moldova has been widely discussed as an option for solving the conflict, with a balanced, multi-entity and multi-ethnic federal state as the end goal. Successful examples of federations, such as Switzerland or Belgium, are easily invoked, even by the Transnistrian leadership (Piehl, 2005, p. 494). Moreover, the longer the *de facto* separation of Bessarabia and Transnistria lasted, the less likely became a straightforward reintegration of Moldova as a unitary nation state, no matter what degree of autonomy would be offered to Transnistria. Thus, some kind of federal and/or ethnic power-sharing solution would appear to be the only way to reintegrate a viable Moldovan state in the near future. This may seem a good alternative to the more radical alternatives of forcing a unitary state structure on the separatists, or dismembering the country altogether. Hence it is not surprising that international actors have at numerous times embraced such approaches. Nonetheless, much depends on the terms under which the federalisation is to take place.

If the federal state were to take the form of a loose confederation or a federation with extensive local autonomy, the *status quo* would be legitimated and prolonged, allowing Transnistria to maintain its *de facto* independence (International Crisis Group, 2004, p. i). The disadvantages of such a loose union can be seen in Bosnia, where two entities have developed state-like structures and only reluctantly engage with one another in their common national institutions at the pressure of the international community. Moreover, the recent independence of Montenegro has shown that asymmetric federations combined with substantial local autonomy of the smaller subject may give strong incentives for secession. Thus, a loose kind of federal union would represent a perpetuation of the *status quo* at best and an intermediary step to an eventual dismemberment "solution" at worst. It is therefore not surprising that both

Transnistria and Russia would welcome such an outcome, whereas Moldova wouldn't accept it.

In fact, any federal solution which includes strong Transnistrian autonomy and/or a Transnistrian veto in key decisions would be likely to put Russia in control of Moldovan internal and foreign politics (Lewis, 2004, p. 223), regardless of whether the Russian troops would be withdrawn or remain as "guarantors" of the federal state. This is by virtue of the pro-Russian orientation of – and Russian influence in – Transnistria. Thus, Russia would still be able to prevent a decisive drift of Moldova towards the West and act freely to secure its interests in Moldova and the wider region. Such an internalisation and institutionalisation of the currently external Russian pressure cannot be the solution. It would do nothing more than turning two already effectively Russian controlled regions into a state with a severe institutional deadlock or even an obedient puppet state, if Transnistrians were to get the upper hand in Moldovan politics again. It was for this reason, that the 2003 Kozak plan was rejected by those Western actors who grasped its implied consequences and ultimately by Moldova itself. There continues to be, however, a widespread lack of understanding of these problems in the academic community and political decision-making circles. This includes – but is not limited to – those who blame US and NATO interests for Moldova's last-minute pullout from what appears to them a viable solution (Hofbauer, 2006, p. 147).

A slightly different approach that focuses more on the process than the final outcome of conflict resolution is that of democratisation, particularly of Transnistria. Democracy is being presented as the cure for the conflict, because of two main arguments: Firstly, it is generally accepted to provide peaceful avenues for the reconciliation of differences by means of debate and compromise. Secondly, it is somehow assumed that the views of the population and the elites in Transnistria are sufficiently different to allow for a quick solution, as soon as politicians representing the "true" interests of the people are elected (OSCE, 2005a/c).

The first may be the case for advanced Western countries with a long democratic history. However, this does not mean that it equally applies to poorer and younger democracies, particularly if coupled with a post-conflict setting. The second argument is also problematic, as Transnistrian leaders to some extent already represent the opinions of the local population, and this is likely to increase with the coming of age of persons who were exclusively or mainly socialised under the separatists' regime. Some observers would even claim that Transnistrian elections are already essentially democratic, or at least on the best way to becoming so (British Helsinki Human Rights Group, 2006).[26] Therefore, it is thinkable that free and fair democratic elections would keep the current leadership in power and give it a further boost for an uncompromising stance. Moreover, even if democratically elected officials would be different individuals that the current leadership, they would not necessarily be better for Moldovan internal relations and its relationship with the West. If Western-infused democracy can bring fiercely anti-Western governments to power in the Middle East, then how can one be certain that it will not put strongly anti-Western, pro-Russian and/or pan-Slavic nationalists in control of Transnistria? Moreover, Moldova itself has deficiencies when it comes to democracy (European Commission, 2004b), and these would only be exacerbated by adding problematic democratic forces from Transnistria to its institutions.

Whilst such pessimistic scenarios may be exaggerated, a fundamental question remains: Where is the sudden democratisation supposed to come from if the current regime does not allow it? And why should the current leadership allow it if they are benefiting from the *status quo* and thus likely to lose out in a democratic reconfiguration of political forces? Proposals, such as the Yushchenko Plan which envisaged truly democratic elections to be held in Transnistria within a matter of months, have no answer to these questions (Nantoi, 2005a). In any

---

[26] However, they often have their own agenda for making such claims. The quoted organisation in particular is a highly controversial "human rights" organisation that has frequently endorsed questionable elections in the former Soviet Union.

case, free and fair elections are but one of the key features of democracy. Others – such as the rule of law and strong democratic institutions – would also have to be established in Transnistria and consolidated in Moldova (Belitser, 2006, p. 20; Körber-Stiftung, 2007, p. 38).

One thing, however, is certain: The perpetuation of the *status quo* is no solution, even though it would suit many people on both sides well. Moldova is not Cyprus, as its economy cannot sustain the artificial division into two unequal parts, and its *status quo* affects neighbouring countries[27] more than that on the Mediterranean island. Therefore, the following chapter and the conclusions will build up to some suggestions on what can be done, with a particular focus on actions that can be taken by the EU.

---

[27] See next chapter

4 The EU and Moldova

4.1 Evolution of relations

For a long time the Soviet Union saw the European Union – then still the European Community (EC) – as an economic appendix of the hostile NATO alliance and therefore had little interest in cooperating with it (Cutler, 1987, p. 261). The Community itself was restricted in its actions with regards to the Soviet Union by Cold War imperatives as well as the incompatible economic systems of the Western and Eastern European blocks. In the last years of the Soviet Union's existence, however, the two parties steered towards closer relations, culminating in the 1988 Joint Declaration on mutual diplomatic recognition and the 1989 Trade and Cooperation Agreement (TCA) which – amongst other things – accorded the Soviet Union with the coveted most favoured nation (MFN) treatment by the EC (Vahl, 2004).

After the break-up of the Soviet Union, technical assistance initially represented a stand-alone approach to the newly-independent states (NIS) (European Commission, 2006). A separate system of Technical Assistance to the Commonwealth of Independent States (TACIS) was set up rather than extending to them the superior PHARE programme that supported the Central European countries in their transition and prepared them for eventual accession to the EU (Baun, 2000, p. 233). TACIS took over seamlessly in 1991 from the 1990 emergency aid programme for the Soviet Union, and funds for Moldova gradually increased. However, these contributions were still relatively small, totalling just over €320 million for the entire period of 1991 to 2006, or an average of about €20 million per year (European Commission, 2007c). Therefore, Moldova was treated as a second class European state at best, or even akin to a third world developing country from which one expected little and which one tried to keep happy by the occasional signing of a cheque. Being small, poor and widely unknown in the West, it was impossible for Moldova to attract a deeper engagement by the EU.

Eventually, Partnership and Cooperation Agreements (PCAs) were concluded to provide the main legal framework for relations between the EU and the NIS and to allow for cooperation beyond technical assistance (European Commission, 2007c). Whilst these were an extension of the EC-Soviet TCA which they replaced, PCAs were not comparable to the Europe Agreements (EAs) offered to Central and Eastern European states (Peers, 1995, p. 829). Therefore, the system of differential cooperation with different parts of Eastern Europe was further cemented. Moreover, the negotiations were not conducted with all CIS states at the same time, thus creating a differentiation within the CIS states as well. This was evidently based on geographical proximity, as the agreements with Russia and the Western NIS were signed before those with more remote CIS states (Fritz, 2005, p. 204).

Moldova, being in the Western CIS category, signed its PCA with the EU in November 1994. The agreement came into force in July 1998, preceded only by those with Russia and Ukraine (European Parliament, 2004). An interim agreement covered the period of 1994 to 1998. Through the PCA, Moldova and the EU granted each other MFN status, and Moldova committed to an approximation of its legislation to that of the EU (Institutul de Politici Publice, 2006). Furthermore, cooperation in numerous areas as well as an eventual free trade area (FTA) was envisaged (Vahl, 2004, p. 173). Notably, the PCA with Moldova is the only one that lacks chapters on the "protection of intellectual, industrial and commercial property and on legislative cooperation" (European Commission, 1994). This can be interpreted as an indication of Moldova's relative unimportance for the EU.

Throughout the 1990s the EU was only half-heartedly engaged in Moldova and hence took several years to replace the old EC-Soviet TCA with the country-specific PCA. Admittedly, the EU was somewhat overwhelmed by the new situation in Eastern Europe. It had only just established formal relations with the Soviet Union when it collapsed and had by definition no experience of dealing directly with the Soviet Republics that had suddenly become independent states. Meanwhile, much attention was diverted to internal developments of the EU such as the completion of the Single Market and the Maastricht Treaty and – towards the end of the decade – increasingly to the Central European neighbour states considered promising candidates for EU enlargement. Therefore, it can be argued that the EU simply did not have the capacity to be engaged with – and in – Moldova on a larger scale. Besides, Moldova must have seemed sufficiently remote from – and economically unimportant to – the EU to be conveniently ignored by decision-makers in Brussels (Wiersma, 2004, p. 195).

Until recently the EU also showed relatively little interest in the Transnistria conflict (Malek, 2006, p. 165). The Yugoslav civil war and the later Kosovo war attracted most of the EU's attention in the security sphere, so that the more distant and smaller Transnistria conflict went almost unnoticed. Already over-reliant on the United States for solving the crises in the Balkans, it would have been almost inconceivable in the 1990s for the EU to take a meaningful initiative in another European conflict, particularly considering that in the case of Transnistria the superpower-turned-regional-power Russia was directly involved.

More recently, however, both the EU's need and its capacity for a more active engagement in Moldova in general and Transnistria in particular have increased. In the early 21st century, the context of the preparations for the 2004 enlargement and the flourishing debates around EU common foreign and security policy (CFSP), lead to plans for greater involvement in the Eastern and Southern neighbourhood aimed at creating a zone of peace and prosperity, via a "ring of friends" around the EU (European Commission, 2003). In 2004 a detailed strategy for the European Neighbourhood Policy (ENP) was developed (European Commission, 2004c). Henceforth, this policy has shaped the EU's relations with Moldova.

In the framework of the ENP, individual country strategies are developed and outlined in country specific action plans. The EU-Moldova action plan lays out priority goals in the areas of democracy, rule of law, media and civic freedoms, judicial reform, cooperation with international financial institutions (IFIs), poverty reduction, economic reforms, fight against corruption and organised crime, border management, trade and migration (European Commission, 2004e). The implementation of these goals is monitored by the joint bodies that were created under the PCA.[28] The key tools for achieving the goals are trade, aid and expert advice:

In addition to the MFN status, Moldova is covered by the EU's Generalised System of Preferences (GSP) and is the only European country to be covered by the new GSP+ scheme since 2005 (European Commission, 2007f). Together, GSP and GSP+ provide many Moldovan goods with privileged access to EU markets in return for protection of labour rights (in the case of GSP), good governance and sustainable development (in the case of GSP+). Indeed, the EU has developed into Moldova's biggest trading partner, which is quite remarkable, as the country had long been a provider of agricultural products for the Soviet Union's internal market, almost completely cut off from neighbouring Romania and the rest of the world. In 2006 the then 25 EU member states accounted for around 35% of Moldova's exports and 31% of its imports, surpassed only by the CIS countries (40% exports / 38% imports) if these are counted collectively (Biroul Naţional de Statistică al Republicii Moldova, 2007b). Since Romania and Bulgaria joined the EU, the trading block accounts for an absolute majority of Moldova's exports (54%) and the largest share of imports (45%) whilst the share of the CIS has declined in terms of exports (34%) and remained constant for imports.[29]

As part of the ENP initiative, in 2007, the European Neighbourhood and Partnership Instrument (ENPI) replaced TACIS, although a number

---

[28] See next section
[29] Based on statistics from the first quarter of 2007 (Biroul Naţional de Statistică al Republicii Moldova, 2007a).

of TACIS projects for Moldova are still running until 2008 (European Commission, 2007e). The ENPI represents a relatively one-sided implementation by the EU of the common goals for Moldova laid out in the 2004 action plan. To achieve these, €209.7 million have been budgeted for the period of 2007-2010, more than doubling the earlier TACIS annual averages to just over €50 million (European Commission, 2007d). Around half of this sum is earmarked for supporting poverty reduction and economic growth. The rest is almost equally divided between promoting democratic development and good governance on the one hand and regulatory reform and administrative capacity building on the other. Increases of these sums and/or other changes in the budget are foreseen in case Moldova performs exceptionally well in terms of governance or if the Transnistria conflict is resolved (European Commission, 2007d).

The ENP in general and the ENPI in particular offer some improvements over earlier arrangements and policies in that they provide for more funds and stronger cooperation between Moldova and the EU. However, at the same time – by virtue of their distinctiveness from other programmes – they reconfirm the differential treatment of Moldova and other states in the "neighbourhood" from those with a clearer accession perspective.[30] The EU is generally silent on the issue of Moldova's accession prospects, yet – when pressed for an answer – it does not categorically rule out such an option for the future (European Commission, 2007g). Meanwhile, the initial 10 years of Moldova's PCA are coming to an end and it is not clear what will replace it. The EU is currently negotiating a new enhanced agreement with neighbouring Ukraine, but nothing comparable is taking place with respect to Moldova. Whilst the EU has traditionally focussed vast proportions of its aid and attention at its immediate neighbours, it remains to be seen whether the Western NIS will

---

[30] Croatia, Macedonia and Turkey have been accorded official candidate country status by the EU, and the label "potential candidate countries" is attached only to Albania, Bosnia and Herzegovina, Montenegro, Serbia and Kosovo (European Commission, 2007b).

enjoy a similar treatment as Central Europe did in the 1990s, or instead suffer from the drawing of a final Eastern border by the EU.

As far as Transnistria is concerned, the EU does not have any formal relations with the self-declared republic by virtue of its non-recognition of this entity. Technically, of course, the EU programmes and agreements with the Republic of Moldova cover the whole country within its internationally recognised boundaries, including Transnistria. In practice, however, the EU's projects, initiatives and funds have seldom extended to Transnistria. Notable exceptions include the EU funding for the reconstruction of a bridge between Moldova and Transnistria that was destroyed in the conflict (European Commission, 2005b, p. 10), as well as trade relations with some Transnistrian companies. In contrast to the OSCE, the EU doesn't treat the Transnistrian authorities as official partners in their own right, and organisations from Transnistria wishing to deal with the European Union have to provide documentation issued by the Moldovan government.

4.2 Agents and agencies

As the EU is a multifaceted multi-level actor, while even a small state like Moldova is not necessarily a coherent unit, it makes sense to also analyse the different kinds of actors involved in the conduct of those relations. On the European Union side, the key actors are EU institutions, missions, individual member states and the private sector. On the Moldovan side, there are different government agencies and economic actors involved in the conduct of bilateral relations. The two sides, furthermore, share joint commissions and monitoring bodies. With such a multitude of actors, there is some scope for conflicts of interests or contradictory approaches.

The European Commission has a *de facto* monopoly over EU diplomacy in that it retains over 120 delegations abroad (European Commission, 2005c), whereas other EU institutions tend to only have representations in accession countries. The Delegation of the European Commission to Moldova was opened as recently as 2005 (European Commission, 2005c). Until then, the Delegation in Kyiv was accredited to all three Western NIS with only TACIS Branch Offices (TBOs) in Chişinău and Minsk. Yet Moldova's case is rather different from that of Belarus which has been very uncooperative towards the EU and until recently rejected the possibility of a full-scale delegation on its territory.[31] Therefore, one is left to conclude that – until the final phase of Romania's accession process – Moldova must have seemed too remote, small and unimportant to deserve a dedicated EU diplomatic mission.

Whereas the day-to-day conduct of bilateral relations is thus firmly in the hands of the Commission's delegations, the Council of the European Union sends special representatives working under the High Representative for CFSP Solana to "troubled regions and countries" such as Moldova (Council of the European Union, 2007). The function of the European Union Special Representative (EUSR) to the Republic of Moldova is to bring Moldova closer to the EU and resolve the Transnistria conflict (Council of the European Union, 2007). The fact that such key functions are fulfilled by the more intergovernmental Council rather than the more supranational Commission means that member states' interests can more directly impact on decisions regarding the Transnistria conflict. Still, EUSR Kálmán Mizsei[32] and his advisers are housed in the Commission's delegations in Chişinău and Kyiv and work in close collaboration with their cohabitants and other EU agencies and programmes in Moldova.

Moreover, despite the lack of clearly defined foreign policy roles and competencies due to the constitutional crisis, all EU institutions pro-

---

[31] The procedures for allowing the opening of a full-scale delegation are now ongoing, due to a recent initiative by Belarusian side.
[32] Mandate ends early 2008.

actively work together on Moldova issues on an informal basis.[33] In order to support the work in the field and keep decision-makers in Brussels informed, both the Commission and the Council Secretariat employ Moldova Desk officers at their headquarters. Yet Moldova and the Transnistria conflict remain much less prominent than the Western Balkans, to which considerable amounts of EU funds and human resources are dedicated. Whilst this appears logical if one considers the large differences in scale between the conflicts in the Balkans and that in Transnistria, a few more resources and a bit more focus could potentially unfreeze the conflict resolution process.

The European Parliament is mainly involved through its Delegation to the EU-Moldova Parliamentary Cooperation Committee, consisting of 14 Members of the European Parliament (MEPs), headed by the Estonian MEP Marianne Mikko. Its annual meetings with the Moldovan counterparts represent fact-finding missions leading to recommendations to both Moldova and the European Commission, but not usually to further actions by the European Parliament itself. The areas covered are EU-Moldovan relations, the Transnistria conflict, visa issues and the goals identified in the EU-Moldova action plan (European Parliament, 2006). If the prospects for Moldovan accession to the EU were to increase dramatically, the European Parliament would most likely play a much bigger role in EU-Moldovan relations, as it did in the relations with the candidates for the recent two rounds of enlargement. However, even in the current situation there may be scope for it to give more legislative advice to aid reforms in Moldova.

The most important EU programmes in Moldova – TACIS/ENPI and EUBAM – are both run by the Commission. The TBO in Chişinău had even been somewhat of an actor in its own right before the Commission's Delegation was opened, a kind of mini-delegation, carrying out more functions than a TACIS department situated within a delegation would have. Technical assistance staff have, however, received instructions from the Delegation in Kyiv and to some extent still continue to do

---

[33] Author's interview with Michael Emerson, 24/03/2007.

so.³⁴ In addition to TACIS, the European Community Humanitarian Office (ECHO) supported the Moldovan health sector for a while (Wiersma, 2004).

EUBAM is a common project with the UNDP – though entirely EU funded – and is headquartered in Odesa. It receives instructions from the EU via the Delegation in the Ukrainian capital. Beyond merely monitoring the border, it gives various types of training to Moldovan and Ukrainian border guards and customs officials and makes suggestions for improving the efficiency and transparency of the border crossings (EUBAM, 2006).

The EU and its member states are also providers of institutional lending and investment for Moldova. Whilst – unlike Russia – Moldova has not received many loans from the European Investment Bank (EIB)³⁵, it has received over €200 million of investments from the European Bank for Reconstruction and Development (EBRD) to which the EU states are major contributors. More than half of this sum has gone to the private sector (EBRD, 2007). These funds are particularly important since other international lending bodies have drastically cut their budgets for Moldova when its reform process stalled and a number of reforms of earlier governments were reversed around the turn of the century (Crowther, 2004b, pp. 41-43).

Individual EU member states are also involved in – and with – Moldova in many different ways. In addition to TACIS/ENPI and EBRD funds, a number of EU member states have provided bilateral support for Moldova, in particular, Denmark, Germany, France, the Netherlands, Sweden and the United Kingdom (Piehl, 2005, p. 517). The latter two were also the initiators of the "New Neighbours Initiative" which lead to the ENP and hence a greater EU involvement in Moldova (Khotin, 2004, p. 144). Romania, Italy and Germany are Moldova's most important trad-

---

[34] The author has gained these and other insights into the functioning of the Commission's Delegations and projects in Kyiv and Chişinău from his internship at the Delegation of the European Commission to Ukraine and Belarus.

[35] The only major investment of the EIB in Moldova is a recently approved €30 million road rehabilitation project (European Investment Bank, 2007).

ing partners in the EU whereas the United Kingdom, France and Luxembourg provide some of the urgently needed investment (Biroul Naţional de Statistică al Republicii Moldova, 2007b; Sturza & Negruţa, 2004).

On the Moldovan side the key body for the conduct of relations with the EU is the Ministry of Foreign Affairs and European Integration which has carried this double name since 2003. Remarkably for a foreign ministry, one of its roles is the coordination of the implementation of European standards *within* Moldova (Ministry of Foreign Affairs and European Integration of the Republic of Moldova, 2006). Other levels of government have departments or individual officials for European affairs, but mostly deal with their national, regional and municipal counterparts in the framework of twinnings and cross-border regional cooperation with neighbouring states.[36] They do, however, deal with EU institutions' representatives directly when it comes to TACIS/ENPI funds.

The role of the Moldovan private sector in the conduct of relations with the EU is rather ambiguous. On the one hand, it is a beneficiary of trade with – and investment – from the Union and represents a significant pro-European driving force in expectation of financial benefits from this orientation (Association for Participatory Democracy, 2002, p. 19). On the other hand, short-term opportunities and vested interests in the Transnistria conflict and trade with Russia and the CIS entice some companies to a more pro-Russian or inconsistent position. Therefore, Moldova's international economic relations mirror those of the political sphere that is oscillating between Russia and the West.

Under the terms of the PCA, the two sides share the aforementioned EU-Moldova Parliamentary Cooperation Committee as well as a Cooperation Council and a Cooperation Committee. The key role of these bodies lies in supervising the implementation of the PCA. Besides, they also provide opportunities for general political dialogue between Moldova and the EU (European Commission, 1994).

---

[36] Authors interview with the Vice Mayor of Cahul, 30/07/2006.

4.3 Issues

The situation in Moldova in general and Transnistria in particular affects the EU in many different ways. Conversely, the EU also has a strong impact on developments in Moldova. Of course, none of this happens in a vacuum, so that there are many links to regional and global politics, some of which are more obvious and more direct than others.

First of all, despite being both small-scale and effectively frozen, the Transnistria conflict poses a number of problems related to military security. Whilst the actual numbers of both Russian and Transnistrian soldiers in Transnistria are relatively low and in any case not directed against European Union territory, any renewed armed conflict between them and Moldova could have spill-over effects into Romania and Ukraine. The biggest threat, however, lies in military equipment piled up in the Russian army's Transnistrian bases, representing the second largest weapons stockpile in Europe (Freedomhouse, 2004). The stocks of Russian weapons and ammunitions easily fall into the wrong hands. Currently material from these stocks, as well as from elsewhere, is already being trafficked from Transnistria to "undesirable destinations" (Emerson, 2001, p. 75) such as civil wars, international conflicts and terrorist organisations, reportedly including the Islamic insurgents in Iraq (Lane, 2007). Thus, the Transnistria conflict – or rather the *status quo* created by it – is already affecting EU nationals caught up in conflicts or involved in conflict resolution attempts abroad and also potentially threatens EU member states in the form of international terrorism. If Russia withdraws its remaining troops without a parallel controlled withdrawal of this equipment, and Transnistrians seize the stocks, these threats would most likely increase.

Moreover, even if access to these stocks of weapons and ammunition is tightly controlled, they pose a number of threats due to their old age. They could simply explode, or set free harmful substances, causing physical destruction and "environmental disaster" (Severin, 2004, p.

163). Whilst the former would most likely affect only the local populations, environmental effects could easily pass to Romania and other nearby EU member states through the air or the rivers Danube and Dniester both of which end in the Black Sea.

Meanwhile, the presence of the Russian army and Moldova's dependence on Russian energy imports do not only freeze the resolution of the Transnistria conflict. They also severely limit Moldova's general political and economic decision-making, as Russia can prevent any undesired developments by means of coercion and threats (Körber-Stiftung, 2005a). Therefore, the EU can never completely rely on Moldova's cooperation and implementation of agreements, no matter how much goodwill is present in Chişinău.

Moldova's economy is severely crippled by the combined effects from Transnistria's control over most of the country's industry and electricity generation facilities and the simultaneous loss of its traditional agricultural markets in the former Soviet Union (Hensel & Gudîm, 2004, p. 89/91). The latter problem was partially engineered by Russia as part of the external dimension of the Transnistria conflict to bring Moldova to its knees and coerce it into a more pro-Russian position.[37] The resulting issues of human security have already affected the EU for many years and are becoming even more pressing since the accession of Romania.

Moldova has earned itself the unfortunate title of "the poorest country in Europe", alongside Albania and is also one of the poorest countries within the CIS (Spanu, 2004). Having such a poor country right on its doorstep is not only contrary to the EU's wish of being surrounded by prosperous peaceful countries (European Commission, 2003), but also creates a number of concrete problems. Most importantly, the economic situation in Moldova has created massive economic migration. An estimated 25% of the workforce (Hensel & Gudîm, 2004, p. 90) is already working abroad. As a lot of this immigration and work is taking place illegally, there is a loss of tax revenue to EU member states and a general lack of control over flows of migrants from Moldova.

---

[37] See above discussion of the Russian blockade of Moldovan wine.

Moreover, whilst Moldovans do not want their country to become part of Romania, large proportions are prepared to accept Romanian citizenship for pragmatic reasons. Hundreds of thousands of Moldovans have already applied for Romanian passports. Since Romania joined the EU the tendency is upwards and could well extend to a majority of the Moldovan population in the near future (Tomiuc, 2007), thereby effectively uniting the populations of Moldova and Romania without uniting their countries. Currently, Romania – which keeps its inclusive citizenship laws in order to justify its claims of Moldova – is being pragmatic by simply not giving out the passports quickly enough.[38] However, if this changes, the EU may be faced with large groups of poor Romanian citizens that were not there when Romania's accession was negotiated. In order to prevent this, the EU made statements to Moldovan media informing the public that Romania's EU accession is not the same as its entry into the Schengen zone.[39] It remains to be seen whether such measures will discourage significant numbers of Moldovans from applying for Romanian passports.

Even those Moldovans who might receive official travel and immigration documents under EU member states' rules often choose to go the illegal route, because it is very stressful and expensive to deal with the embassies accredited to Moldova, which are often located in neighbouring countries or even further away (Guţu & Gheorghiu, 2004, pp. 206-207). This has only been partially addressed by the recent creation of a common visa application centre for six EU member states within the Hungarian embassy, as only two of these countries issue the attractive Schengen visa (Radio Free Europe / Radio Liberty, 2007).

More serious than migrants who stay and work in the EU illegally or try to acquire Romanian and other EU passports are the various types of

---

[38] Only 70,000 Moldovans hold Romanian passports, and despite an estimated stock of 800,000-900,000 applicants, as little as 1,300 passports were given out between August 2005 and August 2006 (Tomiuc, 2007; Şoitu & Şoitu, 2007).

[39] This was witnessed by the author on Romanian language radio stations in Chişinău just before Romania joined the EU, but it probably formed part of a broader information campaign covering different types of media and languages.

criminals and trafficked human beings that pass through Moldova's borders. Besides cheap labour, Moldova is a key "provider" of women and minors for the international sex trade (International Organization for Migration, 2005, p. 6). Many of the trafficked individuals are forced into prostitution by economic circumstances or brute force and often do not know that they are going to work in the sex trade. EU countries are amongst their top destinations, as are the locations of EU missions such as in Kosovo where almost two thirds of trafficked women are believed to be Moldovans (Mîndîcanu, 2004, p. 75). Therefore, it can be argued that the EU has a moral obligation to prevent the trafficking and exploitation of Moldovan women and children. This cannot be done by border security measures and crack-downs in red-light districts alone; there is also a need to address the underlying causes, such as poverty and organised crime.

In addition to arms, illegal immigrants and sex workers, there is considerable trafficking of drugs and other illegal substances as well as smuggling of regular consumer goods at the Moldovan borders (IDIS Viitorul, 2005a, p. 4). The former are an obvious threat to public health in destination countries including EU member states whereas the latter in the best case only cause a loss of tax and customs revenue for the receiving or transit states. However, seemingly regular goods may also pose issues of food security[40] and consumer safety if they pass borders without being checked for their conformity to (EU) safety and quality standards.

In all cases the traffickers are taking advantage of the badly policed borders and generally corrupt border guards, including those of neighbouring countries. EUBAM is therefore a step in the right direction, but by no means enough, as its scale is too limited. In particular it does not cover the Moldovan-Romanian border and does not provide for full-

---

[40] Amongst the most frequently smuggled items at the Transnistrian-Ukrainian border is chicken meat (International Crisis Group, 2006). This highly perishable product passes the border back and forth in quantities that could never be consumed in tiny Transnistria alone. By the time it reaches its end consumers, it may not be safe anymore.

scale Moldovan customs checks. Current tendencies to fortify the EU's external borders attempt to deal with these issues (DW World, 2006), but are unlikely fully to stamp out trafficking and illegal migration. In any case they send a negative signal to the countries supposed to become friendly and prosperous neighbours.

Moreover, corruption and bad policing does not only extend to Moldova's borders. Through its lawlessness and international non-recognition, Transnistria has developed into a refuge for organised crime and individual criminals (International Crisis Group, 2003, p. 6). Conversely, Transnistrian organised crime can operate internationally from its secure home base without fearing prosecution. International arrest warrants have little effect in this unrecognised territory, so that criminals can lead normal public lives there. A good example for this is the head of the Transnistrian youth organisation *Proriv*, Dimitrij Soin, who is wanted by Interpol for murder, but has become somewhat of a celebrity in Tiraspol (Kührer, 2007). Even Moldova proper suffers from relatively weak institutions and flourishing corruption (European Commission, 2007c) so that criminals can easily escape or buy themselves out of prosecution.

Besides such direct impacts on EU member states, the Transnistria conflict and its outcome can potentially have consequences for the EU's general role in its neighbourhood and the rest of the world. Other states in the neighbourhood might turn to Russia, America or even China when they see that the EU is unable to solve the problems of tiny Moldova. The EU remains attractive to its neighbours for economic reasons, but as long as it cannot provide security and does not render sufficient economic assistance, it may drive them into the arms of other geopolitical actors with their own agendas which may be incompatible with that of the EU. It is also questionable how the EU could continue to aspire to be a major global power (European Commission, 2004a) and a leading peacemaker in places such as the Middle East or North Korea if it fails to resolve such a comparatively small conflict at its own doorstep. Combining this with the aforementioned impact of Transnistrian illicit arms trade, the EU could face hard times when it comes to international conflict resolution efforts.

Furthermore, the situation in Transnistria – remote as it may seem from Brussels – is interlinked to many other issues in not always apparent and often contradictory ways.[41] The Kosovo and Montenegro precedents are often cited by Russia as justifications for supporting separatism in its near abroad (Popescu, 2006, p. 7). At the same time, Moscow verbally supports the territorial integrity of Serbia and hypocritically speaks of "dangerous precedents" (Socor, 2007b) set by the violation thereof by Kosovo and the international community. Therefore, whatever the outcome in Kosovo, Russia can bend it for its own purposes. If Kosovo's remains independent, the precedent for Transnistria and others is set. In the unlikely event that Kosovo is returned to Serbia, Russia would have gotten its way in the Balkans, but could still cite the Montenegro precedent for its own purposes in its near abroad, or work towards a federal "Moldova and Transnistria" that could later separate as easily as Serbia and Montenegro did. Finally, if the *status quo* of a partially recognised and internationally supervised Kosovo is prolonged, Russia will most likely continue its contradictory approach to the separatists in the Balkans and its own near abroad. One only needs to compare the case of Transnistria to that of Chechnya to see that Russia does not mind sending out contradictory messages, as long as it benefits from the practice (Hassel, 2006).

In fact, the general EU-Russia relationship is the most important dimension of EU foreign policy that is both affected by and affecting the Transnistria conflict. The list of currently unresolved issues on the EU-Russian agenda is long, and the relations are at a historic low-point, as could be witnessed during the May 2007 EU-Russia summit. Most of the individual issues could be resolved, and the two sides need each other sufficiently enough that they will not allow the relations to deteriorate even further (Segbers, 2007). However, the diverging interests of EU

---

[41] Author's interview with Rosaria Puglisi, 08/12/2006.

member states coupled with a new Russian assertiveness in security, economic and energy issues makes the situation complicated.

Unfortunately, both the EU and some of its member states often worsen the situation by striking deals with Russia that lock out intermediary and transit countries. The most recent example is the construction of the direct gas pipeline from Russia to Germany, that gives Russia more leverage over Belarus and Ukraine – the traditional transit countries (Harks, 2006). Whilst such deals may bring immediate economic benefits, they are eventually dangerous, as they increase dependence on Russian energy and thus give Russia significant leverage over the EU as well (Körber-Stiftung, 2005b). Moreover, by worsening the economic situation in the transit countries in the Western NIS, the aforementioned problems are exacerbated, the impact of which will be felt in the EU.

The EU should therefore rethink its Eastern strategy and build better relationships with Moldova and the other Western NIS, as well as diversifying its energy supplies. In particular, Moldova's dilemma of needing Moscow for the solution of the Transnistria conflict, whilst sincerely wishing for Euro-Atlantic integration, has to be allowed for in the EU's dealing with the country. The choice "either CIS or us" that is sometimes posed by the EU, is neither a real one nor fair, considering the lack of genuine support that accompanies this demand (Stăvilă, 2004, p. 131). Limited aid and investment as well as preferential access of its goods to EU markets, cannot make up for the fact that Moldova's trade balance with the EU is very negative and that the country is hopelessly dependent on Russian energy.

For the moment, Moldova remains explicitly pro-European. Since Moldova was the only CIS country to have been included into the EU-initiated Stability Pact for South-Eastern Europe (SPSEE) that was created in the aftermath of the Kosovo war, it has been encouraged to redefine itself as a South-Eastern European or Balkan country (Neguța & Simionov, 2004, p. 186). It thereby hopes to join the ranks of the former Yugoslavian states with relatively good EU accession prospects rather than being grouped with Ukraine and Belarus which do not have a comparable perspective at the moment. However, such attempts are rebuffed by the EU which insists on treating Moldova within the framework of its relations with CIS states in general and the Neighbourhood Policy in particular (Gheorghiu, 2005a, p. 3). There are of course good reasons for this, as Moldova lags way behind the Western Balkans in its development. Unlike Yugoslavia's successor states, Moldova is not already surrounded by EU member states, so that the debate about its EU accession perspective raises the question of how far eastwards to draw the final border of the EU (Körber-Stiftung, 2005a) in addition to the usual questions about the candidate's capability to meet the criteria for joining and the EU's capacity for further enlargement.

In the long run, however, it is questionable whether the combination of relatively weak incentives and the lack of a clear accession perspective will keep Moldova on a pro-European track. Evidence to the contrary can already be seen in the recent swing-back of the Moldovan president towards a more pro-Russian line. Meanwhile, the mood of the general public could easily follow the route it has done in Turkey, where anti-EU sentiments rise with every day the EU makes no further commitments. Whilst a decline of Moldova's pressure for accession may actually be welcomed by the EU, the side effects of the country turning into a Russian puppet or even a failed state would certainly be felt across its borders.

4.4 The EU and the settlement of the Transnistria conflict

The EU takes its decisions on bilateral issues as well as regional initiatives with the Transnistria conflict in mind and often mentions it explicitly in agreements and other documents. Most recently, it has given the "frozen conflicts" a prominent position in its "Black Sea Synergy" initiative (European Commission, 2007a). Unfortunately, it has taken relatively few actions directly aimed at a resolution of the conflict. It does, of course, take part in the "five-plus-two" conflict resolution negotiations, even if this is only as an observer. However, as Russia is both a participant in the conflict resolution negotiations and a member of the OSCE that chairs the meetings of this format, the process is effectively deadlocked as long as Western and Russian interests diverge in the region. Nonetheless, as the EU is still a relatively new actor in the conflict resolution process and has not (yet) been discredited by a long history of failed attempts, there are several avenues to be explored.

The Union could for example make its own proposals that are acceptable to all parties of the current negotiation format or try to create a new format altogether. Of course, both would be hard even if not impossible. An easier option is gradually to create facts on the ground that lead to a shift to a more favourable situation. The EU has already begun to do that, mainly in the form of assistance to Moldova and negative feedback mechanisms for Transnistria. The former has already been discussed above and in any case is both too limited and not aimed directly enough at the resolution of the Transnistria conflict.

On the negative feedback side, in 2003 the EU issued a travel ban for top Transnistrian officials in order to prevent them from entering the European Union, and in 2004 it added "other persons held responsible for the campaign of intimidation and closure against Latin-script Moldovan schools" to the list (Council of the European Union, 2005). This parallels those actions that were taken against Belarusian and Zimbabwean officials aimed at forcing the leaders to be more conciliatory for personal reasons. It may seem the right approach if one considers that the conflict persists to a large extent due to the personal interest of those banned leaders and their associates. However, the benefits from the *status quo* are likely to be much bigger than the convenience of being able to travel through Europe, and the stigmatisation of these individuals is unlikely to persuade them to adopt a conciliatory stance at the negotiating table. This is particularly the case for the well-off top officials, whereas the lower ranking officials of the group banned in 2004 have since been more cooperative and thus were mostly taken off the EU list (Foreign and Commonwealth Office, 2005).

Even less successful in terms of conflict resolution has been the contribution of EUBAM. It was initially thought that it was possible to resolve the Transnistria conflict by cutting off the supply lines of the illicit activities that Transnistria (Institutul de Politici Publice, 2005). However, the relatively limited scope of EUBAM, coupled with the continuing Russian support for Transnistria has made this impossible. Hence, more recently, this argument has been dropped, and the latest reports hardly mention the Transnistria conflict at all (EUBAM, 2006). This is not to say that there is anything wrong with EUBAM as such, but it is clearly a technical assistance measure and not a tool for a speedy resolution of the conflict.

The big questions that remain therefore regard the scope for a more actively involved EU in the resolution of the Transnistria conflict and the form such involvement could take. Being dependent on both American military security and Russian energy deliveries and without clear foreign policy competences as a result of the constitutional crisis, the EU cannot act freely in the security sphere. Fortunately, as far as Moldova is concerned, the US has no agenda that would be obstructive to that of the EU. Therefore, the "Russian factor" is left as the key external factor to be tackled. Without directly addressing it, an increased EU involvement could easily turn into a "battle of chequebooks" with Russia where each side props up its preferred bank of the Dniester financially (Rothacher, 2005, p. 43). However, this would at best increase the vested interests in the *status quo* and in the worst case escalate the conflict both between Transnistria and Moldova and between Russia and the EU.

It is thus clear that the EU must in some way also engage with Transnistria. Emerson, Noutcheva and Popescu (2007a, p. 3) argue that this could be most effectively done by an "ENP-light" based on so-called "people programmes", positive incentives that win over civil society and the general public through scholarships and other types of funding. In fact, the EU might not have such a hard start, as it is not perceived as an enemy or loathed as much as the OSCE is in Transnistria, ironically despite the fact that Russia is an OSCE member. The socialisation of future generations of Transnistrian elites in EU countries as well as in EU-sponsored programmes in Transnistria could potentially contribute to a true democratisation of the region without bringing anti-Western forces to power.

Of course, Transnistrian elites may want to prevent such developments. However, Transnistrian companies – already rather open to the EU – can be encouraged to apply pressure on the separatist leadership by offering them privileged access to EU funds and markets in return for cooperation. The close connection between Transnistrian big business and politics could bring the latter into line once the EU wins over the former. Meanwhile, the EU's biggest carrot – an accession perspective for Moldova – may be attractive to both parts of Moldova and could thus help to settle the conflict if the EU is prepared to consider it (Lewis, 2004, p. 227).

In this case, the only remaining problem would be posed by Russia. It is and remains the key player, with the potential to obstruct all EU plans by dirty tactics. Therefore, other bargains and reassurances are needed, and the EU has to ensure at all times that its actions are not perceived as threatening Russia. In order to maximise its benefits from its negotiations with Russia, the EU should act with a more unified voice, which may be fully possible only after a resolution of the constitutional crisis. First steps in this direction have been taken, with the old member states increasingly standing by the new members in their quarrels with Russia (Lobjakas, 2007).

5 Conclusions

Moldova certainly seems small and insignificant to most European academics, policy makers and the general public and is therefore not accorded with much attention. Granted, the Transnistria conflict is not a second Bosnia or Kosovo in either scale or substance, nor is Moldova the EU's Mexico in terms of pressure on its outside border. Moreover, the people most affected by the country's conflict, poverty, corruption and organised crime, are certainly Moldovans themselves. Nonetheless, what is going on inside this new direct neighbour does have some significance for the EU and is interconnected with many other issues. This book has endeavoured to raise the general awareness about the country and its conflict as well as the ways in which the EU is affected by – and affecting – the situation.

It was demonstrated that the Transnistria conflict is a complex interplay of history, nationalism, geopolitics and elite interests with the latter two factors dominating despite widely spread beliefs to the contrary. Moreover, it was identified that – whilst the Transnistrian leadership's interests and Moscow's geopolitical calculations are the strongest obstacle to resolving the conflict – vested interests in the *status quo* exist in segments of both sides' societies as well as in third countries such as Ukraine and Russia. Fortunately, these vested interests coupled with the virtual absence of conflict at the personal level and the relatively low manpower of the militaries on both sides make a renewed escalation unlikely if not impossible.

Nonetheless, there are many reasons why the EU should come to the aid of Moldova and help solve the Transnistria conflict. Most importantly, there are a number of EU interests at stake in the conflict. Through the effects of globalisation in general and its new proximity to Moldova in particular, the EU is both actually and potentially affected by the various types of security and criminal threats emanating from the conflict and the *status quo* perpetuated by freezing its solution. In addition to such physical threats posed by the conflict itself, the rampant trade in arms and drugs and other activities of organised crime, there are also issues involved which affect the EU's migration policy as well as its environmental and food security.

Besides, the EU can be said to be morally responsible for Moldova, not only due to its infinitely greater wealth, but also because it aggravates the situation in the country in several ways. This includes often appeasing Russian policy in its near abroad for the sake of an illusory energy security, restrictive visa arrangements that make the lives of ordinary people and small traders harder and last but not least generating demand for the victims of human trafficking. Moreover, if the EU endeavours to be a regional or even global peacemaker and also to spread its prosperity, it might as well start by resolving the conflicts on its doorstep and by propping up its poorest neighbours' economies. Otherwise its credibility might suffer, particularly if it lets down countries with such explicit European aspirations as Moldova.

As this analysis will have made clear, Moldova in general and the Transnistria conflict in particular have not been high on the list of priorities. This has resulted in a rather modest role of the EU in the international conflict resolution process for Transnistria. At the same time, it is apparent that the EU is beginning to be more involved, at least since the preparations for Romania's EU accession and the ENP.

Whilst this involvement is still relatively limited, there are several reasons why there is scope for a more active EU role. Above all, the EU is very attractive to Moldova and other countries in the region due to its soft power. At the same time it is not as objectionable to Russia and Transnistria as other Western actors such as NATO and the United States. In addition, its lack of previous involvement means that the EU has not been discredited by the failures of earlier conflict resolution attempts in the way the OSCE has.

As for the substance of the conflict, geopolitics and elite interests can be more easily manoeuvred and bargained about than historic and nationalist grievances, which are luckily much less important to the conflict than is commonly assumed. All in all, the conflict is probably the easiest to resolve of the frozen conflicts in the post-Soviet world if sufficient time and resources are dedicated to finding a solution.

Nonetheless, several factors will affect the ability of the EU to play a more active role and resolve the Transnistria conflict. Externally, it is dependent upon the United States and Russia for military security and energy deliveries respectively. Whilst the United States has few interfering aims in the region at the moment, it could potentially obstruct the conflict resolution efforts by merely increasing its presence. The key dimension, however, remains that of the – currently difficult – relations between the EU and Russia.

Other external issues such as possible further enlargements or engagements in other conflicts could distract the EU's attention and exert a pull on its resources. At the same time, internal problems such as the EU's constitutional crisis and disagreements between member states about foreign policy priorities make it hard for the EU to speak with a single voice and thus maximise its bargaining power vis-à-vis other geopolitical actors.

There is no guarantee that the EU will become more involved in – or even resolve – the Transnistria conflict in the near future. The new proximity has, however, made this more important, more possible and more likely to be the case. This book has made the case that the EU should act proactively in respect of Moldova and Transnistria rather than to wait for Russia to bully the country back into – or out off – its sphere of influence.

6 Recommendations to the EU

Based on – and rooted in – the preceding analysis, the author offers the following recommendations and considerations to decision makers in the European Union and its member states:

It is clear that attention and resources are needed to address – and also simply to reassess – the Transnistria conflict and the problems related to it as well as to help Moldova out of its desperate general economic situation. As it is a small and poor country with a relatively small conflict, a moderate increase in resources could make a large difference. Increased aid for Moldova – if well targeted – could have a big impact in areas such as democracy, rule of law, social security and civil society. This would also serve to make a common Moldovan state more attractive to Transnistrians. Even drastic increases of the currently very limited aid budget would mean only modest additional commitments for the EU and its member states.

Besides aid, foreign direct investment (fdi) is desperately needed to diversify Moldova's economy and to make its goods competitive and attractive for EU and other markets, thus ending its overdependence on trade with Russia and the CIS. EU investment programmes could help to bring Western funds and knowledge to Moldova by measures such as investment guarantees and information campaigns. Moreover, current general programmes and policies such as the ENP and the Black Sea Synergy initiative, as well as specific measures such as EUBAM need to be expanded and built upon.

With regards to the strategy for resolving the Transnistria conflict, there is no single blue-print or master plan, and the list of failed agreements is already long, so that the focus should be on practical steps – small, but well co-ordinated ones. It is vital, however, that the cross-linkages of the Transnistria conflict with other issues such as the recognition of Kosovo's independence, EU-Russian energy trade and NATO's eastward expansion are taken into account at all times when deciding on particular steps so as to not upset the careful balance of geopolitical forces in the region. At the same time, the cross-linkages also provide an opportunity for bargaining with Russia. The EU should, however, be careful not to sell out its interests in one area for the pursuit of others, or neglect Moldova for gains in other areas, as this would tarnish its image and eventually prove counterproductive.

Of course, the EU will need partners in its conflict resolution efforts. These need to be chosen carefully. In particular, it is advisable to avoid solutions focussed on a strong involvement of NATO or other US dominated organisations in order not to raise Russian and Transnistrian fears. Whilst the US is not as assertive in Moldova as it is in neighbouring Ukraine, the necessity may arrive for the EU to convince it not to push for Moldovan NATO accession for the time being. Equally, the EU should avoid making heavy use of organisations that are either dominated or blocked by Russia, such as the CIS or the OSCE. Less straightforward is the question of involving Moldova's neighbours Romania and Ukraine, as they both have much to contribute due to their historic ties to the involved parties, but also have their own interests that may serve to destabilise the conflict. Therefore, their involvement has to be carefully controlled, and they must not be allowed to hi-jack the process for their own purposes.

The EU also has to keep in mind that Russia would probably not accept the chairmanship of the conflict resolution process to be held by an organisation that it is not a member of, so that the OSCE may have to be kept formally in the chair despite having been discredited by the history of failed resolution attempts. An alternative would be to replace the OSCE with the BSEC, in which case the EU should make strategic use of its newly gained observer status in that organisation. Furthermore, if it is done in a politically sensitive way, the EU can build stronger links with the Western NIS and the pro-Western CIS subgroup GU(U)AM, without threatening Russia, as long as these links occur in the economic rather than the military security sphere.

In any case, Russia itself remains the priority partner and cannot be locked out of the conflict resolution process. As long as Russia is uncompromising, however, the EU has to act unilaterally, taking advantage of local elites' opportunism and calculation by creating economic and other incentives for cooperation and conflict resolution on both sides. In particular, the EU can use its trade relations as a lever and employ an "ENP-light" or "people-directed" approach to Transnistria. This could eventually lead to a rapprochement of Moldova and Transnistria independent of Moscow's input. History would have seen stranger bedfellows than a joint government of Transnistrian ex-Separatists and Moldovan communists. If Russia proves to be compromising, however, far reaching measures would be possible. In cooperation with Russia, the EU could use the full spectrum of its experiences gathered in other conflicts, such as police missions and peacekeeping troops.

All measures borrowed from other contexts have to be adapted for the local contexts, particularly as the cases of Kosovo, Bosnia and Palestine/Israel – unlike the Transnistria conflict – do have strong ethno-religious dimensions. Moreover, past mistakes committed in other conflict resolution attempts should be avoided. In particular, the EU should not sponsor a "Dayton-like" scenario that would create volatile entities with little in common and thus serve to perpetuate separatist aspirations. Also, any federalisation proposals have to be closely examined in order to prevent a subsequent disintegration of Moldova along the lines of Serbia and Montenegro. Disintegration in itself must not be seen as a solution, because it is both unacceptable to the majority of the Moldovan population and has the potential to reignite the conflict in Gagauzia which is less easily separable from the Bessarabian region of Moldova that surrounds it.

In any case, it is best if the EU acts proactively by making its own proposals. These may well build on earlier initiatives, for example in a "Kozak II" approach that attempts to remove the objectionable clauses from what otherwise could have been a decent Russian proposal. As some kind of federal solution will most likely be involved, the EU would have to convince not only Russia, but also Moldova to accept its proposals, due to the negative connotation that the term federalisation has acquired there. This can best be done by including the EU alongside Russia as an official guarantor of the new federal states' sovereignty and territorial integrity as well as by either a complete demilitarisation of Moldova, or the stationing of a more balanced international peace force. In the latter case, it may be possible to create a regionally active international Black Sea peace force with mixed contingents from Russian, Ukrainian, Turkish and EU forces to be used in Moldova and other "frozen conflicts". The joint command could conceivably be put under the auspices of the BSEC.

To help facilitate both general relations with Moldova and a resolution of the Transnistria conflict, EU member states which haven't done so already should consider opening diplomatic representations in Chişinău – as far as this is practicable. Meanwhile, the common EU visa application centre could be extended to all member states who find it impractical to open full scale diplomatic missions at the moment. This would significantly ease the situation for Moldovan citizens wishing to travel abroad and help reduce the demand for illegal access to visas, particularly if combined with visa facilitation measures.

A key decision for the EU will be whether to employ its most effective "golden carrot" by offering a clearer accession perspective to Moldova as a means of resolving the Transnistria conflict and bringing Moldova onto a clearly reform-oriented and pro-Western path. The argument that is often used to justify a postponement of this choice – namely that Moldova first has to choose between Russia and the West and between the CIS and the EU – is rather unfair as it puts Moldova in an impossible situation. In general, there would be nothing wrong with a conditional promise of a true accession perspective as long as the conditions safe-guard the readiness of both the EU and Moldova for the latter's accession.

Eventually, if and when the conflict has been resolved, the EU should try to apply the lessons learned to the other unresolved conflicts in the CIS and beyond, whilst also ensuring that they are adapted to the local circumstances.

7 Update

As this book is going to print, a number of developments are taking place that are of significance to the Transnistria conflict and its solution. Whilst none of them invalidate the line of argument taken here or call for significant changes therein, they ought to instil a sense of urgency in concerned observers:

Directly involving Moldova, there have been renewed minor provocations between Moldova and Transnistria as well as a continuously deteriorating relationship between Bucharest and Chişinău. The latter issue may in fact be the more serious one if it is seen in the context of the Moldovan Communist government's aforementioned swing-back to a more pro-Russian line that has been increasingly apparent since 2006. Growing weaker whilst loosing potential allies puts Moldova in a desperate position that Russia could easily take advantage of. In the absence of substantial international support, Moldova may soon be forced to sell out to Russia, which might entail a virtual loss of sovereignty not only over Transnistria, but over the rest of Moldova as well.

Meanwhile, the EU has abandoned routine border checks between the old member states and the Eastern European new members of the 2004 enlargement round when their full Schengen membership came into force on 21 December 2007. This means that there are now only two controlled borders separating Moldovan people and goods from Western Europe. In the case of bypassing Romania through Ukraine, only one border crossing under EU control has to be passed, unless one overestimates the amount of control exerted by EUBAM over activities in the Moldovan-Ukrainian and Transnistrian-Ukrainian border areas. This makes the issues of trafficking and migration that were raised in this book all the more pressing.

Probably the most significant development, however, is happening neither inside Moldova, nor the EU: Since Kosovo declared its independence from Serbia on 17 February 2008, the world is divided into those states recognising it as an independent state and those which do not, Russia and Moldova falling into the latter category for different reasons. While this book is going to print, it is unclear whether the recognising or non-recognising states will be in the majority, or whether they will both be outnumbered by those not taking a clear position. In any case, the increasingly lively debate over the extent to which the independence of Kosovo creates a precedent for other separatist entities may soon be put to test in the real world, Transnistria being an obvious candidate to attempt following Kosovo's example. This is not to say that an independent Kosovo inevitably brings about an independent Transnistria. After all, the independence of Montenegro has not had such consequences, despite similar talk of a Montenegro precedent. Nonetheless, the EU and Western governments are well advised to carefully consider all the implications before taking further steps with respect to Kosovo that may encourage similar cases elsewhere. Conversely, any actions taken with regards to the Transnistria conflict should avoid making Russia look defeated once again to prevent a further deterioration of EU-Russian relations. Workable compromises will need to be found.

Florian Küchler, February 2008

Bibliography

Abraham, F. (2006). The relations between the USA, the European Union and the OSCE: contributions to international security. Retrieved 30/01/2007, from Studii de securitate: http://www.studiidesecuritate.ro/pdf/c7.pdf

Ascherson, N. (1996). Black Sea: the birthplace of civilisation and barbarism. London: Vintage.

Association for Participatory Democracy. 2002). Adept political commentaries, October-December 2002. Retrieved 30/01/2007, from Policy Documentation Center: http://pdc.ceu.hu/archive/00002648/01/Adept_pol_com_Oct-Dec2002.pdf

Association of the Bar of the City of New York. (2006). Thawing a frozen conflict: legal aspects of the separatist crisis in Moldova. Retrieved 06/01/2007, from Peace Building Framework: http://www.peacebuilding.md/library/147/en/NYCity%20BarTransnistriaReport.pdf

Azi. (2005). By 31 December 2006, Russia Must Withdraw Its Armed Forces from Moldova. Retrieved 22/04/2007, from Moldova.org: http://social.moldova.org/stiri/eng/3225/

BASA-Press. (2006). P.A.C.E. will discuss Moldova's case in February 2007. Retrieved 15/04/2007, from Moldova.org: Politicom: http://politicom.moldova.org/stiri/eng/18927/

Baun, M. J. (2000). A wider Europe: the process and politics of European Union enlargement. Lanham, MD: Rowman & Littlefield Publishers.

Belitser, N. (Ed.). (2006). Trilateral plan for solving the Transnistria issue. Chişinău: Moldova-Ukraine expert group.

Biroul Naţional de Statistică al Republicii Moldova. (2007a). Activitatea de comerţ exterior a Republicii Moldova în trimestrul I 2007. Retrieved 20/05/2007, from Statistica Moldovei: http://www.statistica.md/statistics/dat/962/ro/Activ_com_ext_trimestrul_I_2007.pdf

Biroul Naţional de Statistică al Republicii Moldova. (2007b). Moldova în cifre: breviar statistic. Retrieved 20/05/2007, from Statistica Moldovei: http://www.statistica.md/publications/154/ro/Mold_in_ cifre_2007_breviar_ro_ru.pdf

Blair, A. (2006). Companion to the European Union. Abingdon: Routledge.

Boonstra, J. (2005). From a weak state to a reunified Moldova: new opportunities to resolve the Transdniestria conflict. Retrieved 06/01/2007, from EuroJournal.org: http://eurojournal.org/files/ Boonstra_last_version_oct_05.pdf

Brennan, N. (2003). OSCE dynamics in the "frozen conflict" in Moldova. Retrieved 30/01/2007, from OSCE: http://www.osce.org/documents /mm/2003/09/1867_en.pdf

Brezianu, A., & Spânu, V. (2007). Facts about Transnistria. Retrieved 21/04/2007, from The Moldova Foundation: http://foundation. moldova.org/pagini/eng/767

British Helsinki Human Rights Group. (2006). PMR - presidential elections report. Retrieved 28/04/2007, from British Helsinki Human Rights Group: http://www.bhhrg.org/CountryReport.asp ?CountryID=16&ReportID=269

Bruchis, M. (1997). The Republic of Moldavia: from the collapse of the Soviet empire to the restoration of the Russian Empire. New York: Columbia University Press.

Burla, M. et al. (2005). Transnistrian Market and its Impact on Policy and Economy of the Republic of Moldova. Retrieved 06/01/2007, from Friedrich-Ebert-Stiftung: http://library.fes.de/pdf-files/bueros/ukraine /02934.pdf

Buşcaneanu, S. (2006). How far is the European Neighbourhood Policy a substantial offer for Moldova? Retrieved 22/04/2007, from Association for Participatory Democracy: http://www.e-democracy.md/files/enp-moldova.pdf

Casier, T. (2006). 'Putin's policy towards the West: reflections on the nature of Russian foreign policy'. International Politics, 43, pp. 384–401.

Cavelius, M. (2006). 'Security dynamics in the former Soviet bloc'. Journal of International Relations and Development, 9, pp. 99–102.

Chifu, I. (2004). Basarabia sub ocupatie sovietica: si tentative contemporane de revenire sub tutela Moscovei. Bucharest: Politeia-SNSPA.

Clej, P., & Canţîr, A. (2004). 'The media: struggling to break free from old Soviet habits'. In A. Lewis (Ed.), The EU & Moldova: on a fault-line of Europe. London: Federal Trust. Pp. 55-62.

Cojocaru, G. E. (2001). Politica externa a Republicii Moldova: studii. Chişinău: Civitas.

Coppieters, B., & Emmerson, M. (2002). Conflict resolution for Moldova and Transnistria through federalisation? Retrieved 06/01/2007, from Centre for European Policy Studies: http://shop.ceps.be/downfree.php?item_id=126

Corwin, J. A. (2006). Moldova: Chişinău hopes 'five plus two' will add up to one unitary sate. Retrieved 21/04/2007, from Radio Free Europe / Radio Liberty: http://www.rferl.org/featuresarticle/2006/01/749a29d4-7468-4471-901b-60273f8fa5a5.html

Council of the European Union. (2005). 2640th council meeting: general affairs and external relations. Retrieved 19/05/2007, from The Council of the European Union: http://www.consilium.europa.eu/ueDocs/cms_Data/docs/pressData/en/gena/83885.pdf

Council of the European Union. (2007). EU Special Representatives. Retrieved 18/06/2007, from Council of the European Union: http://www.consilium.europa.eu/cms3_fo/showPage.asp?id=263&lang=EN

Crowther, W. (1997a). 'Moldova: caught between nation and empire'. In I. Bremmer, & R. Taras (Eds.), New states, new politics: building the post-Soviet nations. Cambridge: Cambridge University Press. Pp. 316-349.

Crowther, W. (1997b). 'The politics of democratization in postcommunist Moldova'. In K. Dawisha, & B. Parrott (Eds.), Democratic changes and authoritarian reactions in Russia, Ukraine, Belarus and Moldova. Cambridge: Cambridge University Press. Pp. 282-329.

Crowther, W. (2004a). 'Moldova and Moldovans'. In J. R. MILLAR (Ed.), Encyclopedia of Russian History, Vol. 3. New York: Macmillan Reference USA. Pp. 952-954.

Crowther, W. (2004b). 'Moldova's post-communist transition: ambiguous democracy, reluctant reform'. In A. Lewis (Ed.), The EU & Moldova: on a fault-line of Europe. London: Federal Trust. Pp. 27-48.

CSCE Mission to Moldova. (1993). Report No. 13. Retrieved 30/01/2007, from OSCE: http://www.osce.org/documents/mm/1993/11/454_ en.pdf

CSCE. (1994). Transdniestrian conflict: origins and main issues. Retrieved 30/01/2007, from OSCE: http://www.osce.org/documents /mm/1994/06/455_en.pdf

Cutler, R. M. (1987). 'Harmonizing EEC-CMEA relations: never the twain shall meet?'. International Affairs, 63.2, pp. 259-270.

Deletant, D. (2003). 'The holocaust in Transnistria: an overview in the light of recent research'. (R. Haynes, Ed.) Occasional papers in Romanian studies no.3: Moldova, Bessarabia, Transnistria, pp. 143-162.

Dima, N. (2001). Moldova and the Transdnestr Republic. New York: Columbia University Press.

Dungaciu, D. (2005a). Dileme electorale şi post-electorale la Chişinău. Retrieved 06/01/2007, from Politics-security.info: http://www.politics -security.info/resurse/d37/

Dungaciu, D. (2005b). Moldova ante portas. Bucharest: Tritonic.

Dungaciu, D. (2006). The emerging security environment in the Black Sea area: strategic options for Romania and Moldova. Retrieved 06/01/2007, from Studii de securitate: http://www.studiidesecuritate.ro/pdf/c2.pdf

DW World. (2006). Romania Beefs Up Security at EU's Eastern Frontier. Retrieved 27/05/2007, from DW World: http://www.dw-world.de/dw/article/0,2144,2287371,00.html

EBRD. (2007). Moldova: EBRD country factsheet. Retrieved 10/06/2007, from EBRD: http://www.ebrd.com/pubs/factsh/country/moldova.pdf

Emerson, M. (2001). Redrawing the map of Europe. Basingstoke: Palgrave.

Emerson, M. et al. (2006). European Neighbourhood Watch 22. Brussels: Centre for European Policy Studies.

Emerson, M. et al. (2007a). European Neighbourhood Policy two years on: time indeed for an 'ENP plus'. Brussels: Centre for European Policy Studies.

Emerson, M. et al. (2007b). European Neighbourhood Watch 26. Brussels: Centre for European Policy Studies.

EUBAM. (2006). Annual Report: European Union Border Assistance Mission to Moldova and Ukraine 2005/2006. Odesa: EUBAM.

European Centre for Minority Issues. (2006). Background. Retrieved 30/01/2007, from European Centre for Minority Issues: http://ecmi.de/emap/download/Moldova_Background.pdf

European Commission. (1994). Partnership and Cooperation Agreement. Retrieved 06/01/2007, from European Commission: http://ec.europa.eu/comm/external_relations/ceeca/pca/pca_moldova.pdf

European Commission. (2003). Wider Europe — neighbourhood: a new framework for relations with our Eastern and Southern neighbours. Retrieved 30/01/2007, from European Commission: http://ec.europa.eu/world/enp/pdf/com03_104_en.pdf

European Commission. (2004a). A world player: the European Union's external relations. Brussels: European Commission.

European Commission. (2004b). European neighbourhood policy: country report Moldova. Retrieved 06/01/2007, from European Commission: http://ec.europa.eu/world/enp/pdf/country/moldova_ enp_country_report_2004_en.pdf

European Commission. (2004c). European neighbourhood policy: strategy paper. Retrieved 29/04/2007, from European Commission: http://ec.europa.eu/world/enp/pdf/strategy/strategy_paper_en.pdf

European Commission. (2004d). Proposal for a regulation of the European Parliament and of the Council laying down general provisions establishing a European Neighbourhood and Partnership Instrument. Retrieved 06/01/2007, from European Commission: http://ec.europa.eu/world/enp/pdf/com04_628_en.pdf

European Commission. (2004e). Proposed EU/Moldova Action Plan. Retrieved 06/01/2007, from Europa: www.europa.eu .int/comm/world/enp/pdf/action_plans/Proposed_Action_Plan_EU-Moldova.pdf

European Commission. (2005a). Europäische Nachbarschaftspolitik: ein Jahr des Fortschritts. Retrieved 06/01/2007, from Europa: http://europa.eu/rapid/pressReleasesAction.do?reference=IP/05/14 67&format=PDF&aged=1&language=DE&guiLanguage=en

European Commission. (2005b). European Union assistance to Eastern Europe, the Caucasus and Central Asia: transport. Retrieved 17/06/2007, from European Commission: http://ec.europa .eu/europeaid/projects/tacis/publications/information/thematic_tran sport_en.pdf

European Commission. (2005c). The Delegation's mandate. Retrieved 17/06/2007, from The European Commission's Delegation to the Republic of Moldova: http://www.delmda.ec.europa.eu/about_ us/1_en.html

European Commission. (2006). The EU's relations with Eastern Europe & Central Asia: TACIS. Retrieved 10/06/2007, from European Commission: http://ec.europa.eu/external_relations/ceeca/tacis/index.htm

European Commission. (2007a). Black Sea Synergy – bringing the region closer to the EU. Retrieved 25/04/2007, from Europa: http://www.europa.eu/rapid/pressReleasesAction.do?reference=IP/07/486&format=HTML&aged=0&language=EN&guiLanguage=en

European Commission. (2007b). Candidate and potential candidate countries. Retrieved 29/04/2007, from European Commission: http://ec.europa.eu/enlargement/countries/index_en.htm

European Commission. (2007c). European neighbourhood and partnership instrument: Republic of Moldova country strategy paper 2007-2013. Retrieved 14/04/2007, from European Commission: http://ec.europa.eu/world/enp/pdf/country/enpi_csp_moldova_en.pdf

European Commission. (2007d). European neighbourhood and partnership instrument Republic of Moldova: national indicative programme 2007-2010. Retrieved 17/05/2007, from European Commission: http://ec.europa.eu/world/enp/pdf/country/enpi_nip_moldova_en.pdf

European Commission. (2007e). TACIS national action programme (NAP) 2003: on-going. Retrieved 29/04/2007, from The European Commission's Delegation to the Republic of Moldova: http://www.delmda.ec.europa.eu/en/eu_and_moldova/NAP2003-2005ALL-WEB.pdf

European Commission. (2007f). The EU's relations with Moldova. Retrieved 28/04/2007, from European Commission: http://ec.europa.eu/comm/external_relations/moldova/intro/index.htm#assistance_

European Commission. (2007g). The policy: what is the European neighbourhood policy? Retrieved 10/06/2007, from European Commission: http://ec.europa.eu/world/enp/policy_en.htm

European Investment Bank. (2007). Moldova European Roads. Retrieved 10/06/2007, from European Investment Bank: http://www.eib.europa.eu/projects/pipeline/project.asp?pipe=1814&listing=1&Country=156

European Parliament. (2004). Russia and the other countries of the former Soviet Union. Retrieved 28/04/2007, from European Parliament: http://www.europarl.europa.eu/facts_2004/6_3_4_en.htm

European Parliament. (2005). Plan for the settlement of the Transdniestrian problem. Retrieved 24/04/2007, from European Parliament: http://www.europarl.europa.eu/meetdocs/2004_2009/documents/fd/dmd20050621_07/dmd20050621_07en.pdf

European Parliament. (2006). EU-Moldova parliamentary cooperation committee: ninth meeting. Retrieved 19/05/2007, from European Parliament: http://www.europarl.europa.eu/meetdocs/2004_2009/documents/pv/640/640714/640714en.pdf

Fodor, H. (Ed.). (1995). Belarus and Moldova: country studies. Washington: Library of Congress.

Foreign and Commonwealth Office. (2005). Statement by the Presidency of the European Union concerning restrictive measures against the leadership of the Transnistrian region of Moldova. Retrieved 10/06/2007, from UK presidency of the EU: http://www.eu2005.gov.uk/servlet/Front?pagename=OpenMarket/Xcelerate/ShowPage&c=Page&cid=1107293561746&a=KArticle&aid=1133773457484&date=2005-12-12

Fowler, J. (1991). Charter of the Commonwealth of Independent States [Unofficial translation]. Retrieved 14/06/2007, from theRussiaSite.org: http://www.therussiasite.org/legal/laws/CIScharter.html

Freedomhouse. (2004). Transnistria [Moldova]. Retrieved 26/05/2007, from Freedomhouse: http://www.freedomhouse.org/modules/mod_call_dsp_country-fiw.cfm?year=2004&country=3080

Fritz, V. (2005). 'New divisions in Europe? East–East divergence and the influence of European Union enlargement'. Journal of International Relations and Development, 8, pp. 192–217.

Gabanyi, A. U. (2004). Die Republik Moldau im Kontext der neuen EU-Nachbarschaftspolitik. Retrieved 06/01/2007, from Stiftung Wissenschaft und Politik: http://www.swp-berlin.org/common/get_document.php?id=1094

Ghebali, V.-Y. (2005). 'Growing pains at the OSCE: the rise and fall of Russia's pan-European expectations'. Cambridge Review of International Affairs, 18.3, pp. 375-388.

Gheorghiu, V. (2004). What part should the EU play in the improvement of the economical and political situation of the Republic of Moldova? Retrieved 06/01/2007, from Institutul de Politici Publice: www.ipp.md/public/biblioteca/73/en/RoleEU~01.07.04.doc

Gheorghiu, V. (2005a). EU-Moldova Action Plan: Negotiations and Implementation. Retrieved 06/01/2007, from Institutul de Politici Publice: www.ipp.md/public/biblioteca/92/ro/Yerevan272.doc

Gheorghiu, V. (2005b). Moldova on the way to the European Union: distance covered and next steps to be done. Retrieved 06/01/2007, from Institutul de Politici Publice: http://www.ipp.md/public/biblioteca/83/en/MoldovaWayEU.pdf

Gherman, N. (2003). 'Transnistria since 1990 as seen from Chişinău'. (R. Haynes, Ed.) Occasional papers in Romanian studies no.3: Moldova, Bessarabia, Transnistria, pp. 181-188.

Government of the Republic of Moldova. (2005). Internal report on semestrial evaluation of the EU-Moldova action plan implementation. Retrieved 06/01/2007, from Central and Eastern European Online Library: http://www.ceeol.com/aspx/getdocument.aspx?logid=5&id=88a123cc-882d-4841-ad55-9209e673bcee

Gribincea, M. (2001). The Russian policy on military bases: Georgia and Moldova. Oradea: Editura Cogito.

Guțu, O., & Gheorghiu, V. (2004). 'River Prut: a softer iron curtain?'. In A. Lewis (Ed.), The EU & Moldova: on a fault-line of Europe. London: Federal Trust. Pp. 203-210.

GUUAM. (2000). The GUUAM group: history and principles. Retrieved 11/06/2007, from GUUAM: Geogria Ukraine Uzbekistan Azerbaijan Moldova: http://www.guuam.org/general/history.html

Hækkerup, H. (2005). 'Russia, the OSCE and post-Cold-War European security'. Cambridge Review of International Affairs, 18.3, pp. 371-373.

Hanne, G. (1998). Der Transnistrien-Konflikt: Ursachen, Entwicklungsbedingungen und Perspektiven einer Regulierung. Munich: Carl Hanser Verlag.

Hanne, G. (2004). 'The "Dniester Moldovan Republic": building an authoritarian state'. In A. Lewis (Ed.), The EU & Moldova: on a fault-line of Europe. London: Federal Trust. Pp. 79-86.

Harks, E. (2006). 'The conundrum of energy security in Eastern and Western Europe'. The EU and the Eastern neighbours: democracy and stabilization without accession? [Conference Papers].

Hassel, F. (2006). 'Mit Volksbefragungen will der Kreml seine Macht sichern'. Frankfurter Rundschau, 16/09/2006, p.6.

Hausleitner, M. (Ed.). (2001). Rumänien und der Holocaust: zu den Massenverbrechen in Transnistrien 1941 - 1944. Berlin: Metropol.

Hensel, S., & Gudîm, A. (2004). 'Moldova's economic transition: slow and contradictory'. In A. Lewis (Ed.), The EU & Moldova: on a fault-line of Europe. London: Federal Trust. Pp. 89-101.

Hill, W. (2005). Keynote Address. Retrieved 22/04/2007, from Südosteuropa Gesellschaft: http://www.suedosteuropa-gesellschaft.com/pdf_2005/moldova/key_notes/hill.pdf

Hofbauer, H. (2003). Osterweiterung: vom Drang nach Osten zur peripheren EU-Integration. Vienna: Promedia.

Hofbauer, H. (2006). Mitten in Europa: politische Reiseberichte aus Bosnien-Herzegowina, Belarus, der Ukraine, Transnistrien/Moldawien und Albanien. Vienna: Promedia.

Hopmann, P. T. (2003). 'Managing conflict in post-Cold War Eurasia: the role of the OSCE in Europe's security "architecture"'. International Politics, 40, pp. 75–100.

Huntington, S. (1997). The clash of civilizations and the remaking of world order. New York: Touchstone.

IDIS Viitorul. (2005a). Political and security statewatch, nr. 6. Retrieved 06/01/2007, from IDIS Viitorul: http://www.politics-security.info/resurse/d115/

IDIS Viitorul. (2005b). Political and security statewatch, nr. 7. Retrieved 06/01/2007, from IDIS Viitorul: http://www.politics-security.info/resurse/d117/

Institutul de Politici Publice. (2005). Establishing joint border checkpoints on the Transnistrian sector of the Moldova-Ukraine border. Retrieved 06/01/2007, from Institutul de Politici Publice: http://www.ipp.md/public/biblioteca/96/en/JBC%20versiune%20site%20eng1.pdf

Institutul de Politici Publice. (2006). European Strategy of the Republic of Moldova. Retrieved 22/04/2007, from Institutul de Politici Publice: http://www.ipp.md/biblioteca1.php?l=en&id=85

International Crisis Group. (2003). Moldova: no quick fix. Retrieved 06/01/2007, from International Crisis Group: http://www.crisisgroup.org/library/documents/report_archive/A401086_12082003.pdf

International Crisis Group. (2004). Moldova: regional tensions over Transnistria. Retrieved 06/01/2007, from International Crisis Group: http://www.crisisgroup.org/library/documents/europe/moldova/157_moldova_regional_tensions_over_transdniestria.pdf

International Crisis Group. (2006). Moldova's uncertain future. Retrieved 06/01/2007, from International Crisis Group: http://www.crisisgroup.org/library/documents/europe/moldova/175_moldova_s_uncertain_future.pdf

International Organization for Migration. (2005). Second annual report on victims of trafficking in South-Eastern Europe: country report: the Republic of Moldova. Retrieved 26/05/2007, from International Organization for Migration: Moldova: http://www.iom.md/materials/rts_en.pdf

Ionescu, D. (2002). From SSMR to the Republic of Moldova ± pmr. Chişinău: Museum.

Jakubiak, M. (Ed.). (2006). Prospects for EU-Moldova economic relations. Warsaw: Centre for Social and Economic Research.

Katchanovski, I. (2006). Cleft countries: regional political divisions and cultures in post-Soviet Ukraine and Moldova. (A. Umland, Ed.) Stuttgart: ibidem.

Kempe, I. (1998). Direkte Nachbarschaft: Die Beziehungen zwischen der erweiterten EU und der Russischen Föderation, Ukraine, Weißrußland und Moldova. Gütersloh: Verlag Bertelsmann Stiftung.

Khotin, R. (2004). 'Moldova and Ukraine: pro-western guarantor to the east'. In A. Lewis (Ed.), The EU & Moldova: on a fault-line of Europe. London: Federal Trust. Pp. 143-148.

Khudoley, K. (2003). 'Russia and the European Union: new opportunities, new challenges'. In A. Moshes (Ed.), Rethinking the respective strategies of Russia and the European Union. Moscow: Carnegie Moscow Center.

King, C. (1995). Post-Soviet Moldova: a borderland in transition. London: Royal Institute of International Affairs.

King, C. (2000). The Moldovans: Romania, Russia, and the politics of culture. Stanford, CA: Hoover Institution Press.

Körber-Stiftung. (2005a). Frontiers and horizons of the EU: the new neighbours Ukraine, Belarus and Moldova. Hamburg: edition Körber-Stiftung.

Körber-Stiftung. (2005b). Russland und der Westen: Chancen für eine neue Partnerschaft. Hamburg: edition Körber-Stiftung.

Körber-Stiftung. (2007). Das Schwarze Meer zwischen der EU und Rußland: Sicherheit, Energie, Demokratie. Hamburg: edition Körber-Stiftung.

Kotkin, S. (2001). Armageddon Averted: the Soviet Collapse, 1970–2000. Oxford: Oxford University Press.

Küchler, F. (2007a). 'Book Review of I. Katchanovski, "Cleft countries" and H. Pirchner, Jr, "Reviving Greater Russia?"'. Cambridge Review of International Affairs, 20.1, pp. 195-198.

Küchler, F. (2007b). Moldawien: Probleme mit Religionsfreiheit [Interview Recording]. Retrieved 05/03/2007, from Vatican Radio: http://www.oecumene.radiovaticana.org/ted/Articolo.asp?c=121440

Küchler, F. (2007c). Resolving the Transnistria conflict: Ukrainian national security interest vs. vested economic interests. Retrieved 05/06/2007, from Natsionalni Interesy Ukrayini: http://national-interests.com.ua/index.php?option=com_vfm&Itemid=26&do=download&file=conference+materials|Sbornik+statey.doc

Kührer, F. (2007). Transnistrien: Brücke für einen geeinten Kontinent von Wladiwostok bis Dublin? Retrieved 26/05/2007, from Eurasisches Magazin: http://www.eurasischesmagazin.de/artikel/?artikelID=20070313

Laitin, D. D. (1998). Identity in formation: the Russian-speaking populations in the near abroad. London: Cornell University Press.

Lane, G. (2007). Iraq's secret weapons supplier. Retrieved 26/05/2007, from CBN: http://www.cbn.com/CBNnews/123505.aspx

Lewis, A. (Ed.). (2004). The EU & Moldova: on a fault-line of Europe. London: Federal Trust.

Lobjakas, A. (2007). EU: bloc seeks 'single voice' in dialogue with Russia. Retrieved 27/05/2007, from Radio Free Europe / Radio Liberty: http://www.rferl.org/featuresarticle/2007/05/3B69F900-1715-48E6-9369-5D65A32A6562.html

Löwenhardt, J. (2004). 'The OSCE, Moldova and Russian Diplomacy in 2003'. The Journal of Communist Studies and Transition Politics, 4, pp. 103-112.

Malek, M. (2006). 'Der Konflikt im Dnjestr-Gebiet (Moldova)'. In W. Feichtinger, & P. Jureković (Eds.), Internationales Konfliktmanagement im Fokus: Kosovo, Moldova und Afghanistan im kritischen Vergleich. Baden-Baden: Nomos. Pp. 139-185.

Manners, I. J. (1999). Creating a stable peace beyond the 'paper curtain': the European Union and Moldova. Retrieved 06/01/2007, from European Consortium for Political Research: http://www.essex.ac.uk/ecpr/events/jointsessions/paperarchive/mannheim/w7/manners.pdf

Meurs, W. P. van. (1994). The Bessarabian question in communist historiography: nationalist and communist politics and history-writing. New York: East European Monographs.

Meurs, W. P. van. (2002). 'Romanen'. In T. M. Bohn, & D. Neutatz (Eds.), Studienhandbuch östliches Europa, Band 2: Geschichte des Russischen Reiches und der Sowjetunion. Köln: Böhlau.

Mîndîcanu, A. (2004). 'Not a happy one: woman's lot in Moldova'. In A. Lewis (Ed.), The EU & Moldova: on a fault-line of Europe. London: Federal Trust. Pp. 73-77.

Ministry of Foreign Affairs and European Integration of the Republic of Moldova. (2005). Report of the government of the Republic of Moldova on the implementation of the EU-Moldova Action Plan (August-October 2005). Retrieved 06/01/2007, from Ministry of Foreign Affairs and European Integration of the Republic of Moldova: http://www.mfa.md/En/EurInteg/Documents/RAPORT%20aug-octob2005.pdf

Ministry of Foreign Affairs and European Integration of the Republic of Moldova. (2006). European Integration. Retrieved 10/06/2007, from Ministry of Foreign Affairs and European Integration of the Republic of Moldova: http://www.mfa.md/european-integration/

Nantoi, O. (1999). Report on the problem of internally displaced persons in the Republic of Moldova [paper]. Chişinău: UNHCR.

Nantoi, O. (2002). The east zone conflict in the Republic of Moldova: a new approach [paper]. Chişinău: Institutul de Politici Publice.

Nantoi, O. (2003). External factors and the prospects of Moldovean state [paper]. Chişinău: Institutul de Politici Publice.

Nantoi, O. (2005a). The plan for the Transnistrian conflict settlement proposed by Ukraine: pros and cons [paper]. Chişinău: Institutul de Politici Publice.

Nantoi, O. (2005b). Transnistrian conflict: what could the European Union and the United States of America do? Retrieved 06/01/2007, from Institutul de Politici Publice: www.ipp.md/public/comentarii/ 39/en/Transnistrian%20Conflict-EU%20and%20SUA_Engl29.doc

Neguţa, A., & Simionov, A. (2004). 'Moldova and the EU: a view from Chişinău'. In A. Lewis (Ed.), The EU & Moldova: on a fault-line of Europe. London: Federal Trust. Pp. 185-194.

Neukirch, C. (2004). 'Moldova's eastern dimension'. In A. Lewis (Ed.), The EU & Moldova: on a fault-line of Europe. London: Federal Trust. Pp. 133-142.

Nikolaidis, A. (2005). European neighbourhood policy. EU and Ukraine: "neighbour, partner, member?". Retrieved 06/01/2007, from Hellenic Foundation for European & Foreign Policy: http://www.eliamep.gr/eliamep/files/PN05.08.pdf

Obuah, E. (2006). 'Combating global trafficking in persons: the role of the United States post-September 2001'. International Politics, 43, pp. 241–265.

Oertel, B. (2005). 'Go West mit Hammer und Sichel'. Die Tageszeitung 05-06/03/2005, p. 5.

OSCE. (1997). The Moscow Memorandum. Retrieved 30/01/2007, from OSCE: http://www.osce.org/documents/mm/1997/05/456_en.pdf

OSCE. (1998). Odessa Agreement. Retrieved 30/01/2007, from OSCE: http://www.osce.org/documents/mm/1998/03/457_en.pdf

OSCE. (1999). Joint statemept of participants in the Kiev meeting on issues of normalisation of relations between the Republic of Moldova and Transdniestria. Retrieved 30/01/2007, from OSCE: http://www.osce.org/documents/mm/1999/07/458_en.pdf

OSCE. (2003). OSCE dynamics in the "frozen conflict" in Moldova. Retrieved 30/01/2007, from OSCE: http://www.osce.org/documents/mm/2003/09/1867_en.pdf

OSCE. (2004). Proposals and recommendations Of the mediators from the OSCE, the Russian Federation, Ukraine with regards to the Transdniestrian settlement. Retrieved 30/01/2007, from OSCE: http://www.osce.org/documents/mm/2004/02/2079_en.pdf

OSCE. (2005a). Appeal of the Parliament of the Republic of Moldova "on promoting the criteria of democratization in the Transnistrian region of the Republic of Moldova". Retrieved 22/04/2007, from OSCE: http://www.osce.org/documents/sg/2005/06/15296_en.pdf

OSCE. (2005b). Assessment visit to the Transdniestrian region of the Republic of Moldova. Retrieved 30/01/2007, from OSCE: http://www.osce.org/documents/rfm/2005/03/14036_en.pdf

OSCE. (2005c). Declaration by the Parliament of the Republic of Moldova on the initiative of Ukraine regarding the settlement of the Transdniestrian conflict. Retrieved 22/04/2007, from OSCE: http://osce.org/documents/sg/2005/06/15295_en.pdf

OSCE. (2005d). Joint declaration by the mediators in the Transdniestrian settlement from the OSCE, Russian Federation and Ukraine. Retrieved 30/01/2007, from http://www.osce.org/documents/mm/2005/08/15974_en.pdf

OSCE. (2005e). Joint statement by the mediators in the negotiations process toward a political settlement of the Transdniestrian problem from the OSCE, the Russian federation, and Ukraine. Retrieved 30/01/2007, from OSCE: http://www.osce.org/documents/mm/2005/01/4126_en.pdf

OSCE. (2005f). On the consultations of the mediators in the Transdniestrian settlement from the OSCE, the Russian Federation, and Ukraine with the representatives of the republic of Moldova and Transnistria. Retrieved 30/01/2007, from OSCE: http://www.osce.org/documents/mm/2005/01/4162_en.pdf

OSCE. (2005g). On the Meeting of mediators from OSCE, Russian Federation and Ukraine with political representatives of Republic of Moldova and Transdniestria. Retrieved 30/01/2007, from European Centre for Minority Issues: http://www.ecmimoldova.org/fileadmin/ecmimoldova.org/docs/transd.official/OSCE,%20Russian%20and%20Ukraine%20Meeting-18.05.2005.pdf

OSCE Permanent Council. (1999). Decision no. 329. Retrieved 30/01/2007, from OSCE: http://www1.osce.org/documents/pc/1999/12/2517_en.pdf

Ozhiganov, E. (1997). 'The Republic of Moldova: Transdniester and the 14th army'. In A. Arbatov, A. Chayes, A. Handler Chayes, & L. Olson (Eds.), Managing conflict in the former Soviet Union: Russian and American perspectives. Cambridge, MA: Harvard University. Pp. 145-209.

PACE. (2007). Council of Europe: Parliamentary Assembly. Retrieved 15/04/2007, from PACE: the Parliamentary Assembly of the Council of Europe: http://assembly.coe.int/Communication/Brochure/Bro01-e.pdf

Peers, S. (1995). 'From Cold War to lukewarm embrace: the European Union's agreements with the CIS states'. The international and comparative law quarterly, 44.4, pp. 829-847.

Piehl, E. (2005). 'Die Republik Moldau'. In E. Piehl, P. W. Schulze, & H. Timmermann (Eds.), Die offene Flanke der Europäischen Union: Russische Föderation, Belarus, Ukraine und Moldau. Berlin: BWV. Pp. 459-530.

Pinder, J., & Shishkov, Y. (2002). The EU & Russia: the Promise of Partnership. London: Federal Trust.

Pirchner, Herman, Jr. (2005). Reviving Greater Russia?: The future of Russia's borders with Belarus, Georgia, Kazakhstan, Moldova and Ukraine. Oxford: University Press of America.

Pop, A. (2003). 'The Conflict in the Transnistrian Region of the Republic of Moldova'. (R. Haynes, Ed.) Occasional papers in Romanian studies no.3: Moldova, Bessarabia, Transnistria, pp. 205-217.

Popescu, N. (2004). Europeanization and conflict resolution: a view from Moldova. Retrieved 06/01/2007, from European Centre for Minority Issues: http://ecmi.de/jemie/download/1-2004Comment02.pdf

Popescu, N. (2005). Occasional Paper n° 60: The EU in Moldova – Settling conflicts in the neighbourhood. Retrieved 06/01/2007, from European Union Institute for Security Studies: http://www.iss-eu.org/occasion/occ60.pdf

Popescu, N. (2006). "Outsourcing" de facto statehood: Russia and the secessionist entities in Georgia and Moldova. Brussels: Centre for European Policy Studies.

Pridnestrovie.net. (2006). What's in a name: "Pridnestrovie" vs "Transnistria". Retrieved 10/06/2007, from pridnestrovie.net: http://www.pridnestrovie.net/name.html

Protsyk, O., Volentir, A., & Bucătaru, I. (2007). Addressing the Transnistrian conflict: competing stances of Moldova's political parties and expert community. Retrieved 05/03/2007, from European Centre for Minority Issues: http://www.ecmi.de/download/working_paper_37_en.pdf

Radio Free Europe / Radio Liberty. (2007). Six EU states create visa center in Moldova. Retrieved 26/05/2007, from Radio Free Europe / Radio Liberty: http://www.rferl.org/featuresarticle/2007/04/4F6426 D6-C83B-4278-AF0B-1731B667F233.html

Rothacher, A. (2005). 'Moldawien: Auswanderung statt Demokratie'. KAS-Auslands-Informationen, 5, pp. 32-43.

Ryan, K. (2006). Ethnic Moldovans in Pridnestrovie prefer independence over unification with Moldova. Retrieved 18/06/2007, from Tiraspol Times: http://www.tiraspoltimes.com/node/179

Schneider, E. (2005). 'Die ukrainische Außenpolitik unter Wiktor Juschtschenko'. Vestnik analitiki, 3, pp. 97-113.

Segbers, K. (2007). Zum Streit zwischen der EU und Russland: Polnisches Fleisch ist kein Kernproblem der Weltpolitik. Retrieved 27/05/2007, from Tagesschau.de: http://www.tagesschau.de/ aktuell/meldungen/0,1185,OID6753736_TYP6_THE_NAV_REF1_ BAB,00.html

Serebrian, O. (2004). '"Good brothers", bad neighbours: Romanian/Moldovan relations'. In A. Lewis (Ed.), The EU & Moldova: on a fault-line of Europe. London: Federal Trust. Pp. 149-153.

Severin, A. (2004). 'Moldova and the OSCE: a history of failed initiatives'. In A. Lewis (Ed.), The EU & Moldova: on a fault-line of Europe. London: Federal Trust. Pp. 161-168.

Skvortova, A. (2003). Moldova and the EU: direct neighbourhood and security issues. Retrieved 06/01/2007, from Moldova.org: http://www.moldova.org/download/eng/288/

Socor, V. (2005a). Poroshenko drafts, Yushchenko launches a plan for Transnistria. Retrieved 18/04/2007, from Eurasia Daily Monitor: http://www.jamestown.org/publications_details.php?volume_id=407 &issue_id=3312&article_id=2369652

Socor, V. (2005b). Unedifying debut to 5+2 negotiations on Moldova. Retrieved 18/04/2007, from Eurasia Daily Monitor: http://www.jamestown.org/edm/article.php?article_id=2370415

Socor, V. (2006). Solana gaffe overshadows failure of 5+2 negotiations. Retrieved 21/04/2007, from http://www.jamestown.org/edm/ article.php?article_id=2370844

Socor, V. (2007a). Moldovan president changing tone and negotiators with Russia on Transnistria. Retrieved 21/04/2007, from Eurasia Daily Monitor: http://politicom.moldova.org/stiri/eng/41296/

Socor, V. (2007b). Reading and misreading Moscow's positions on Kosovo. Retrieved 27/05/2007, from Eurasia Daily Monitor: http://www.jamestown.org/print_friendly.php?volume_id=420&issue _id=4057&article_id=2372072

Şoitu, D., & Şoitu, C. T. (2007). 'January 1st on both sides of the Prut river'. EUDIMENSIONS Newsletter, 2, pp. 3-5.

Solana, J. (2006). The role of the EU in promoting and consolidating democracy in Europe's east. Retrieved 06/01/2007, from European Commission's Delegation to Georgia: http://www.delgeo.cec.eu.int/en/press/060503%20VILNIUS%20spe ech.html

Solzhenitsyn, A. I. (1995). The Russian question at the end of the twentieth century. London: The Harvill Press.

Soros Foundation-Moldova. (2005). Transnistrian conflict – status quo and prospects. Retrieved 06/01/2007, from Institutul de Politici Publice: http://www.ipp.md/public/biblioteca/86/en/Soros%20200511_English.doc

Spanu, V. (2004). 'Why is Moldova poor and economically volatile?'. In A. Lewis (Ed.), The EU & Moldova: on a fault-line of Europe. London: Federal Trust. Pp. 103-111.

Spinner, M. (2003). Civil war and ethnic conflict in post-Soviet Moldova: the cases of Gagauzia and Transnistria compared. Retrieved 18/06/2007, from GRIN Publishing: http://www.grin.com/en/preview/13303.html

Springborg, R. et al. (2007). European Neighbourhood Watch 23. Brussels: Centre for European Policy Studies.

Stati, V. (2003). Dictionar moldovenesc - românesc. Chişinău: Biblioteca Pro-Moldova.

Stăvilă, I. (2004). 'Moldova between east and west: a paradigm of foreign affairs'. In A. Lewis (Ed.), The EU & Moldova: on a fault-line of Europe. London: Federal Trust. Pp. 127-132.

Sturza, I., & Negruţa, V. (2004). 'Foreign aid, trade and investment: inconsistent policies'. In A. Lewis (Ed.), The EU & Moldova: on a fault-line of Europe. London: Federal Trust. Pp. 113-123.

Sysoyev, G. (2007). Popping the bubble: when a self-proclaimed republic gets too big for its britches. Retrieved 08/04/2007, from Kommersant: http://www.kommersant.com/p756525/r_520/ Moldova,_Transdniestr,_Abkhazia,_South_Ossetia/

Tavares, R. (2004). 'Contribution of macro-regions to the construction of peace: a framework for analysis'. Journal of International Relations and Development, 7, pp. 24-47.

Tcaci, I. (2005). Trilateral model for Moldova. Retrieved 06/01/2007, from Eurojournal.org: http://eurojournal.org/files/0510tcaci-1.pdf

Teague, E. (2004). 'Moldova: a brief history'. In A. Lewis (Ed.), The EU & Moldova: on a fault-line of Europe. London: Federal Trust. Pp. 13-24.

Tomiuc, E. (2007). Moldova: No Signs Of Feared Mass Migration To EU. Retrieved 26/05/2007, from Radio Free Europe / Radio Liberty: http://www.rferl.org/featuresarticle/2007/03/981C2D5B-44E7-49EE-9B99-693D80177116.html

Troebst, S. (2003). "'We are Transnistrians!": Post-Soviet identity management in the Dniester valley'. Ab Imperio: Theory and history of nationalism and empire in the post-Soviet space, 2003(1), pp. 437-466.

U.S. Department of State. (2004). Moldova: international religious freedom report 2004. Retrieved 11/03/2007, from U.S. Departmentg of State Website: http://www.state.gov/g/drl/rls/irf/2004/35473.htm

U.S. Department of State. (2005). The U.S. and the Transnistrian conflict. Retrieved 21/04/2007, from USINFO: http://usinfo.state.gov/eur/Archive/2005/Sep/27-7547.html

United Press International. (2007). Moldovan separatists vote on independence. Retrieved 18/06/2007, from United Press International: http://www.upi.com/NewsTrack/Top_News/2006/09/17/moldovan_separatists_vote_on_independence/1521/

Vahl, M. (2004). 'The EU and Moldova: a neglected relationship'. In EU & Moldova: on a fault-line of Europe. London: Federal Trust. Pp. 171-183.

Vahl, M., & Emerson, M. (2004). 'Moldova and the Transnistrian conflict'. In B. Coppieters, M. Emerson, M. Huysseune, T. Kovridze, G. Noutcheva, N. Tocii, et al., Europeanization and conflict resolution – case studies from the European periphery. Gent: Academia Press. Pp. 149-180.

Voronin, V. (2005). Wir wollen Europa in Moldova errichten. Retrieved 06/01/2007, from Botschaft der Republik Moldau in Berlin: http://www.botschaft-moldau.de/de/aktuelles.html

Waters, T. R. (2002). The "Moldovan Syndrome" & the re-Russification of Moldova forward into the Past! Surrey: Conflict Studies Research Centre.

Waters, T. R. (2003). 'Security concerns in post-Soviet Moldova: the roots of instability'. (R. Haynes, Ed.) Occasional papers in Romanian studies, 3: Moldova, Bessarabia, Transnistria, pp. 189-203.

Weidenfeld, W. (2001). Beyond EU Enlargement. Retrieved 06/01/2007, from Centrum für angewandte Politikforschung: http://www.cap.uni-muenchen.de/download/2001/EUk-eg.PDF

Wiersma, J. M. (2004). 'Moldova and the European Union: a missed opportunity?'. In A. Lewis (Ed.), The EU & Moldova: on a fault-line of Europe. London: Federal Trust. Pp. 195-201.

Wilde, A. (2006). Die neuen Nachbarn der EU - Ukraine, Belarus, Moldau: Politische und gesellschaftliche Entwicklungen. Retrieved 12/02/2007, from Gesellschaft Sozialwissenschaftlicher Infrastruktureinrichtungen e.V.: http://www.gesis.org/Information/SowiNet/sowiOnline/NachbarnEU/NacbarnEU_gesamt.pdf

Young Fine Gael. (2005). 'The enlarged EU's relations with the Russian Federation, Ukraine, Belarus and Moldova: "European regions united"'. The Vulcan, II.I.3, pp. 22-26.

Zaporojan-Pirgari, A. (2004). 'Minority rights in Moldova: consolidating a multiethnic society'. In A. Lewis (Ed.), The EU & Moldova: on a fault-line of Europe. London: Federal Trust. Pp. 63-72.

Zellner, W. (2005). 'Russia and the OSCE: from high hopes to disillusionment'. Cambridge Review of International Affairs, 18.3, pp. 389-402.

Index

Abkhazia 28, 72
accession to the Russian Federation 55, 65-66, 75
Adjaria 28
agriculture 84, 92
aid 81, 84-85, 97, 103, 107
Albania 85, 92
anti-EU orientation 98
anti-Moldovan orientation 44
anti-Romanian orientation 44-45
anti-Russian orientation 41-42, 43, 53
anti-Semitism 42-43
anti-Western orientation 78, 101
arms trade 91, 94-95, 104
assimilation 36, 40
authoritarianism 44, 52
autonomy 31, 37, 60, 76-77
Azerbaijan 71
Balkans 21, 56, 83, 88, 96-98
Băsescu, Traian 70
Belarus 27, 56, 87, 89, 97, 99
Belgium 76
Bessarabia 31-32, 34, 40, 43, 45-47, 49-52, 63, 76, 109
Bessarabian independence 49
Bessarabian Orthodox Church 42-43
bilateral negotiations 71, 75
Black Sea 22, 27-28, 49, 56, 70, 72, 92, 98, 107, 110
Black Sea Synergy 98, 107
blockade 52, 54, 68, 92
border controls 68, 113
border crossings 89, 113
border guards 47, 89, 94
border management 84
border security 94
Bosnia 21, 76, 85, 103, 109
Brussels 83, 88, 96

BSEC 60, 72, 108, 110
Bucharest 44, 113
Bulgaria 22, 27, 70, 84
Bulgarians 34, 36
Cahul 90
ceasefire 33, 60, 61
census 34
Central Europe 81-83, 86
Chechnya 28, 96
chicken meat 94
China 95
Chişinău 36-38, 40, 44, 63, 68, 70, 87-89, 92-93, 110, 113
citizenship 34, 55, 65-66, 93
civic freedoms 84
civil society 53, 75, 100, 107
civil war 28, 31, 33, 45, 50, 83, 91
civilisations 48-49, 52
Cold War 64, 81
Commonwealth of Independent States (CIS) 33, 38, 56, 60, 71, 74, 82, 84, 90, 92, 97-98, 107-108, 110-111
communism 43, 50, 109, 113
Communist Party of Moldova 64, 113
Communist Party of the Soviet Union 33
confederation 76
conflict resolution 28-29, 47-48, 56-57, 59, 61-68, 70-72, 74-77, 88, 91-92, 96, 99-101, 103-105, 107-110, 113
consumer safety 94
corruption 46, 50, 84, 94-95
Cossacks 55
Council of Europe (CoE) 73-74
Council of the European Union 87-88

Crimea 67
Croatia 85
CSCE 60, 62
culture 34-35, 51-52, 57
customs 89, 94-95
Cyprus 79
Cyrillic script 35-36, 38-39, 41
Czechoslovakia 21
Danube river 92
Davis, Terry 73
Dayton accords 109
demilitarisation 110
democracy 44, 75, 77-79, 84-85, 107
democratic elections 33, 78
democratisation 73, 76, 77-78, 101
Denmark 89
deportation 42, 49
détente 73
DHL 54
discrimination 42
disengagement 60
disintegration 109
dismemberment 31, 75-76
division of Moldova 47
Dniester river 31-32, 42-45, 49, 52, 63, 92, 100
Donne, John 21
drug trafficking 94, 104
Eastern Europe 27, 81-82, 113
EC Delegation to Moldova 87-89
EC Delegation to Ukraine and Belarus 22-23, 87-89
education 37-39, 41, 99
election observation 75
elites 31, 45-46, 49-52, 57, 68, 77, 101, 103-104, 109
embargo 64
Emerson, Michael 67, 73, 88, 100
energy 54, 56, 68, 92, 97, 100, 104-105, 107

entities 65, 72, 76, 86, 109, 114
environmental security 104
ethnic cleansing 34, 45, 47
ethnic conflict 33, 40, 43-48, 57
ethnicity 33-36, 40, 43-49, 109
EU accession 22, 27, 81, 84-85, 87-88, 92-93, 97-98, 101, 104, 110
EU Border Assistance Mission (EUBAM) 75, 88-89, 94, 100, 107, 113
EU borders 22, 86, 95, 98, 103, 113
EU common foreign and security policy (CFSP) 83
EU constitutional crisis 87, 100, 101, 105
EU enlargement 27, 83, 88, 98, 105, 113
EU foreign policy 87, 96, 100, 105
EU member states 27, 29, 71, 84, 86-87, 89, 91-95, 97-98, 101, 105, 107, 110, 113
EU neighbourhood 22, 83, 85, 95
EU peacekeeping forces 109-110
EU police missions 109
EU visa application centre 93, 110
EU-Moldova action plan 84-85, 88
EU-Moldova Parliamentary Cooperation Committee 88, 90
EU-Moldovan relations 83, 86-88, 90, 97, 110
Euro-Atlantic integration 27, 70, 97
Europe Agreements (EAs) 82
European Bank for Reconstruction and Development (EBRD) 89

European Commission 23, 87-89
European Community (EC) 81
European Community
  Humanitarian Office (ECHO)
  89
European Court of Human Rights
  (ECHR) 74
European Investment Bank (EIB)
  89
European Neighbourhood and
  Partnership Instrument (ENPI)
  84-85, 88-90
European Neighbourhood Policy
  (ENP) 83-85, 89, 98, 100, 104,
  107, 109
European Parliament 88
European Union (EU) 22, 27, 28-
  29, 47, 50, 56, 62, 64, 67, 70-
  75, 79, 81-101, 103-105, 107-
  110, 113-114
European Union Special
  Representative (EUSR) 50, 87
EU-Russia summit 96
EU-Russian relations 28, 96,
  100, 105, 107, 114
EU-Soviet relations 81, 83
EU-Transnistrian relations 86
extremism 43, 46, 51
federalisation 61, 64, 70-71, 73,
  76, 109, 110
five-plus-two negotiations 62, 99
food security 94, 104
forced prostitution 94
foreign direct investment (fdi)
  107
France 89-90
free trade area (FTA) 82
frozen conflicts 28, 47, 72, 91,
  98, 105, 110
Gagauz people 34-36, 42
Gagauz language 37
Gagauzia 31-32, 37, 109
Gagauzian independence 32-33

Gazprombank 55
Generalised System of
  Preferences (GSP) 84
geography 31, 57, 82
geopolitics 22, 27, 52, 55, 57,
  75, 95, 103-105, 108
Georgia 27, 71
Germany 42, 89, 97
ghettoisation 45
globalisation 103
good governance 84-85
Gorbachev, Mikhail 33
Greater Romania 35, 70
GU(U)AM 71-72, 108
High Representative for CFSP
  87
Hill, Christopher 22-23
history 31, 33, 35-36, 47-49, 51-
  52, 57, 59, 64, 99, 103-104,
  108-109
history textbooks 35
hot phase 32-33, 45-47, 55, 59
human rights 74-75, 78
human security 92
human trafficking 94-95, 104
Hungary 93
Huntington, Samuel 48-49, 52
ideology 50
immigration 34, 84, 92-95, 104,
  113
imperialism 44-45, 60, 70, 73
industry 46, 49-50, 54, 82, 92
Ingushetia 28
interethnic communication 37-38
intermarriage 38, 45
international community 72, 76,
  96
international financial institutions
  (IFIs) 84
international law 65
international organisations 38,
  56, 59, 70-71, 74-75
International Red Cross 75

Interpol 95
investment 54, 89-90, 97, 107
Iraq 21, 70, 91
irredentism 35, 68, 70
Islam 91
Israel 109
Istanbul summit agreement 61
Italy 89
Jehovah's Witnesses 43
Jews 36, 42, 44
judicial reform 84
Katchanovski, Ivan 49, 52
Kosovo 28, 55, 83, 85, 94, 96-97, 103, 107, 109, 113-114
Kosovo war 83, 97
Kozak plan 61, 70, 77, 109
Kurdish Iraq 21
Kyiv 28, 50, 67, 69, 87-89
labour rights 84
language 22, 34-39, 41, 43-46
Latin script 41, 43, 99
Lebanon 21
Lebed, Alexander Ivanovich 55-56
legislative cooperation 82
Lenin, Vladimir Ilyich 36
Luxembourg 90
Maastricht Treaty 83
Macedonia 85
market access 84, 97, 101
media 27-29, 37-38, 47, 50, 84, 93
Mediterranean 79
Members of the European Parliament (MEPs) 88
Mexico 103
Middle East 78, 95
Mikko, Marianne 88
military security 74, 91, 100, 105, 108
minority languages 36
Minsk 87

Moldova 21-23, 25, 27-29, 31-38, 41-52, 54-57, 59-68, 70-79, 81-101, 103-105, 107-110, 113-114
Moldovan ASSR 31
Moldovan citizenship 34-35
Moldovan economy 34, 52, 79, 92, 107
Moldovan forces 32, 45, 47
Moldovan foreign policy 45, 48, 77
Moldovan government 32-33, 54, 60, 65, 70, 73, 86, 90, 113
Moldovan independence 31-33, 41-44, 48-49, 68
Moldovan language 35-36, 39, 41
Moldovan Ministry of Foreign Affairs and European Integration 90
Moldovan nation 35
Moldovan nationalism 31
Moldovan Orthodox Church 42-43
Moldovan parliament 33, 60
Moldovan police 32, 47
Moldovan politics 48, 57, 77
Moldovan Popular Front 33, 43-44, 46
Moldovan sovereignty 31-33, 44, 59, 71, 110, 113
Moldovan SSR 31, 33, 49
Moldovan television 37
Moldovan territorial integrity 59-61, 64, 71, 110
Moldovan wine 54, 92
Moldovanism 35
Moldovan-Romanian border 94
Moldovan-Romanian relations 68, 113
Moldovan-Russian relations 71
Moldovans 31-32, 35, 47, 51, 93, 103, 109-110, 113

Moldovan-Transnistrian border 47, 74
Moldovan-Transnistrian relations 61
Moldovan-Ukrainian border 67-68, 75, 89, 113
Molotov-Ribbentrop Pact 31
Montenegro 55, 76, 85, 96, 109, 114
Moscow 31, 35, 48, 52, 55, 61, 63, 65-67, 96-97, 103, 109
most favoured nation (MFN) status 81-82, 84
multilateral conflict resolution 62
multilateral negotiations 71
Muslims 43
Nagorno Karabakh 28, 72
national heroes 35, 37, 51
nationalism 28, 46, 48, 60, 78, 103, 105
nation-building 35
NATO 27-28, 56, 74, 77, 81, 104, 107-108
NATO accession 27, 74, 108
NATO expansion 28, 56, 108
NATO member states 27
NATO Partnership for Peace 74
Netherlands 89
neutrality 55, 59-60, 62, 74
New Neighbours Initiative 89
newly-independent states (NIS) 81-82, 85, 87, 97, 108
NGOs 75
non-believers 43
normalisation of relations 61
North Korea 95
occupation 31
Odesa 28, 61, 89
Odesa agreement 61
Orange Revolution 27, 52-53, 69
organised crime 84, 94-95, 103-104

orthodox Christianity 31, 42-43, 48
Orthodox Church 42, 45
OSCE 61-62, 70-74, 86, 99, 101, 104, 108
Ossetia 28, 72
Ottoman Empire 31
Palestine 109
pan-Romanianism 46
paramilitary forces 32
Parcani agreements 60
Parliamentary Assembly of the Council of Europe (PACE) 73
Partnership and Cooperation Agreements (PCAs) 82, 84-85, 90
peacekeeping 47, 64-67, 72, 74, 109-110
peasants 32, 38
perestroika 33, 41
PHARE 81
pipelines 72, 97
political culture 49, 52
Pora 53
poverty 78, 82, 84-85, 92-94, 103-104, 107
power-sharing 46, 50, 76
Primakov Memorandum 61
private sector 86, 89-90
privatisation 54
pro-European orientation 90, 97-98
property rights 82
Proriv 52-53, 73, 95
pro-Romanian orientation 41, 43
pro-Russian orientation 31, 40, 45, 48, 53, 64, 67-69, 71, 73-74, 77-78, 90, 92, 98, 113
pro-Western orientation 45, 64, 67-69, 74, 108, 110
Prut river 31
public opinion polls 43

quadrilateral negotiations 60-62, 71
radio 38, 93
rapprochement 109
recognition of Transnistria 28, 65, 86, 95
referendum 47, 75
reforms 41, 49, 84-85, 88-89, 110
refugees 32
regionalism 50-52
reintegration 65, 76
religion 41, 43, 109
religious conflict 45
restitution 42
reunification 43, 47, 63, 68, 93
Roma 36
Romance languages 41
Romania 22, 27, 29, 31, 34-35, 37, 42-43, 47, 49, 51, 57, 59-60, 62, 65, 68, 70, 84, 87, 89, 91-93, 104, 108, 113
Romanian citizenship 93
Romanian language 35-39, 41, 43-45, 93
Romanian Orthodox Church 43
Romanian television 37
Romanianisation 31, 46, 60
Romanian-Moldovan dictionary 35
Romanians 34-36, 38, 40-46, 49, 51, 73
rule of law 79, 84, 107
Russia 27-29, 33, 37, 47-48, 51-52, 54-57, 59-68, 70-75, 77-78, 82-83, 89-92, 95-101, 103-105, 107-110, 113-114
Russian 14th Army 32-33, 44, 55, 61
Russian citizenship 55, 65-66
Russian civil war 31
Russian Duma 61

Russian Empire 31, 35-36, 40, 49
Russian language 28, 36-41, 45-46
Russian military 47, 52, 55-56, 60-62, 66-67, 74, 77, 91-92, 110
Russian military bases 67, 91
Russian near abroad 27, 67, 70, 96, 104
Russian Orthodox Church 42
Russian television 37
Russian-Belarusian relations 56
Russian-Moldovan friendship treaty 61
Russians 31, 34-35, 38-40, 42, 44-46, 49, 51
Rwanda 21
Schengen zone 93, 113
secession 51, 76
self-determination 41, 65
separatism 28, 32-33, 42-43, 45, 51, 53, 55, 59-60, 63, 65, 67, 71-76, 78, 96, 101, 109, 114
Serbia 21, 85, 96, 114
Serbo-Croatian 34
Sevastopol port 56
sex trade 94
Single Market 83
Slavs 35, 45, 51, 60, 78
Smirnov, Igor Nikolaevich 46
smuggling 94
Snegur, Mircea 33
socialisation 78, 101
soft power 55, 104
Soin, Dimitrij 95
Solana, Javier 87
South Ossetia 72
South-Eastern Europe 56, 97
Soviet coat-of-arms 39
Soviet nationality politics 41

Soviet Union 28, 31-36, 39-40, 42, 44, 49, 56, 64, 68, 73, 78, 81, 83-84, 92
sphere of influence 65, 105
Stability Pact for South-Eastern Europe (SPSEE) 97
state of emergency 33
state-building 35
Stephen the Great 37
superpower 83
sustainable development 84
Suvorov, Alexander Vasilyevich 37
Sweden 89
Switzerland 76
TACIS Branch Offices (TBOs) 87-88
Tajikistan 28
technical assistance 81-82, 88, 100
Technical Assistance to the Commonwealth of Independent States (TACIS) 81, 84-85, 87-90
terrorism 91
Tighina/Bendery 32
Tiraspol 32, 37, 39-40, 51, 53-55, 61, 73, 95
trade 38, 50, 54, 56, 68, 72, 81-82, 84, 86, 90, 94-95, 97, 104, 107, 109
Trade and Cooperation Agreement (TCA) 81-82
Transnistria 21-23, 25, 28-29, 31-34, 39-57, 59-68, 70-79, 83, 85-88, 90-92, 94-101, 103-105, 107-110, 113-114
Transnistria conflict 21, 28-29, 31-34, 43-44, 47-48, 50, 52, 55-57, 59, 63, 66-68, 70-74, 83, 85, 87-88, 90-92, 95-98, 100, 103-105, 107, 109-110, 113-114

Transnistrian coat-of-arms 39-40
Transnistrian elections 73, 75, 78
Transnistrian forces 45, 47, 66, 91
Transnistrian independence 31-33, 44-45, 55, 59, 61-63, 65, 75-76, 114
Transnistrian opposition 65
Transnistrian politics 57
Transnistrian regime 39-41, 44-45, 52, 55, 65, 78, 86, 99, 103
Transnistrian Rouble 65
Transnistrians 32, 44, 49-50, 55, 57, 63, 67-68, 74, 77, 91, 101, 107
Transnistrian-Ukrainian border 94, 113
travel ban 99
trilateral negotiations 62, 71
Tripartite Commission of Control 60
Turkey 85, 98, 110
twinning 90
Ukraine 27-29, 31, 38, 40, 42, 47, 49, 52-54, 56, 59-62, 67-68, 71, 74, 82, 85, 89, 91, 97, 103, 108, 110, 113
Ukrainian Communist Party 68-69
Ukrainian language 28, 38-39, 41
Ukrainian Party of Regions 68-69
Ukrainian Socialist Party 68-69
Ukrainian SSR 31
Ukrainian-Russian relations 67
Ukrainians 34-36, 38, 40, 42, 49, 51, 60
UNDP 75, 89
unilateralism 66-67, 109
United Kingdom 89-90
United Nations (UN) 65, 74-75

United States of America (USA) 62, 70, 73, 77, 83, 95, 100, 104-105, 108
Uzbekistan 71
vested interests 44, 46, 50, 52, 68, 90, 100, 103
visa 88, 93, 104, 110
volunteers 32, 44, 55
Voronin, Vladimir 50, 52, 64, 70, 98
Washington 70
weapon stocks 66, 91

Western Europe 21, 27-28, 81, 113
World War II 31, 49
Yedinstvo (Unity) movement 31, 33
Yeltsin, Boris 33
Yugoslav civil war 45, 83
Yugoslavia 27-28, 34, 45, 83, 97-98
Yushchenko Plan 67, 78
Yushchenko, Viktor 67-68, 78
zadira politics 67
Zimbabwe 99

SOVIET AND POST-SOVIET POLITICS AND SOCIETY

Edited by Dr. Andreas Umland

ISSN 1614-3515

1   *Андреас Умланд (ред.)*
    Воплощение Европейской
    конвенции по правам человека в
    России
    Философские, юридические и
    эмпирические исследования
    ISBN 3-89821-387-0

2   *Christian Wipperfürth*
    Russland – ein vertrauenswürdiger
    Partner?
    Grundlagen, Hintergründe und Praxis
    gegenwärtiger russischer Außenpolitik
    Mit einem Vorwort von Heinz Timmermann
    ISBN 3-89821-401-X

3   *Manja Hussner*
    Die Übernahme internationalen Rechts
    in die russische und deutsche
    Rechtsordnung
    Eine vergleichende Analyse zur
    Völkerrechtsfreundlichkeit der Verfassungen
    der Russländischen Föderation und der
    Bundesrepublik Deutschland
    Mit einem Vorwort von Rainer Arnold
    ISBN 3-89821-438-9

4   *Matthew Tejada*
    Bulgaria's Democratic Consolidation
    and the Kozloduy Nuclear Power Plant
    (KNPP)
    The Unattainability of Closure
    With a foreword by Richard J. Crampton
    ISBN 3-89821-439-7

5   *Марк Григорьевич Меерович*
    Квадратные метры, определяющие
    сознание
    Государственная жилищная политика в
    СССР. 1921 – 1941 гг
    ISBN 3-89821-474-5

6   *Andrei P. Tsygankov, Pavel
    A.Tsygankov (Eds.)*
    New Directions in Russian
    International Studies
    ISBN 3-89821-422-2

7   *Марк Григорьевич Меерович*
    Как власть народ к труду приучала
    Жилище в СССР – средство управления
    людьми. 1917 – 1941 гг.
    С предисловием Елены Осокиной
    ISBN 3-89821-495-8

8   *David J. Galbreath*
    Nation-Building and Minority Politics
    in Post-Socialist States
    Interests, Influence and Identities in Estonia
    and Latvia
    With a foreword by David J. Smith
    ISBN 3-89821-467-2

9   *Алексей Юрьевич Безугольный*
    Народы Кавказа в Вооруженных
    силах СССР в годы Великой
    Отечественной войны 1941-1945 гг.
    С предисловием Николая Бугая
    ISBN 3-89821-475-3

10 *Вячеслав Лихачев и Владимир
    Прибыловский (ред.)*
    Русское Национальное Единство,
    1990-2000. В 2-х томах
    ISBN 3-89821-523-7

11 *Николай Бугай (ред.)*
    Народы стран Балтии в условиях
    сталинизма (1940-е – 1950-е годы)
    Документированная история
    ISBN 3-89821-525-3

12 *Ingmar Bredies (Hrsg.)*
    Zur Anatomie der Orange Revolution
    in der Ukraine
    Wechsel des Elitenregimes oder Triumph des
    Parlamentarismus?
    ISBN 3-89821-524-5

13 *Anastasia V. Mitrofanova*
    The Politicization of Russian
    Orthodoxy
    Actors and Ideas
    With a foreword by William C. Gay
    ISBN 3-89821-481-8

14 Nathan D. Larson
    Alexander Solzhenitsyn and the
    Russo-Jewish Question
    ISBN 3-89821-483-4

15 Guido Houben
    Kulturpolitik und Ethnizität
    Staatliche Kunstförderung im Russland der
    neunziger Jahre
    Mit einem Vorwort von Gert Weisskirchen
    ISBN 3-89821-542-3

16 Leonid Luks
    Der russische „Sonderweg"?
    Aufsätze zur neuesten Geschichte Russlands
    im europäischen Kontext
    ISBN 3-89821-496-6

17 Евгений Мороз
    История «Мёртвой воды» – от
    страшной сказки к большой
    политике
    Политическое неоязычество в
    постсоветской России
    ISBN 3-89821-551-2

18 Александр Верховский и Галина
    Кожевникова (ред.)
    Этническая и религиозная
    интолерантность в российских СМИ
    Результаты мониторинга 2001-2004 гг.
    ISBN 3-89821-569-5

19 Christian Ganzer
    Sowjetisches Erbe und ukrainische
    Nation
    Das Museum der Geschichte des Zaporoger
    Kosakentums auf der Insel Chortycja
    Mit einem Vorwort von Frank Golczewski
    ISBN 3-89821-504-0

20 Эльза-Баир Гучинова
    Помнить нельзя забыть
    Антропология депортационной травмы
    калмыков
    С предисловием Кэролайн Хамфри
    ISBN 3-89821-506-7

21 Юлия Лидерман
    Мотивы «проверки» и «испытания»
    в постсоветской культуре
    Советское прошлое в российском
    кинематографе 1990-х годов
    С предисловием Евгения Марголита
    ISBN 3-89821-511-3

22 Tanya Lokshina, Ray Thomas, Mary
    Mayer (Eds.)
    The Imposition of a Fake Political
    Settlement in the Northern Caucasus
    The 2003 Chechen Presidential Election
    ISBN 3-89821-436-2

23 Timothy McCajor Hall, Rosie Read
    (Eds.)
    Changes in the Heart of Europe
    Recent Ethnographies of Czechs, Slovaks,
    Roma, and Sorbs
    With an afterword by Zdeněk Salzmann
    ISBN 3-89821-606-3

24 Christian Autengruber
    Die politischen Parteien in Bulgarien
    und Rumänien
    Eine vergleichende Analyse seit Beginn der
    90er Jahre
    Mit einem Vorwort von Dorothée de Nève
    ISBN 3-89821-476-1

25 Annette Freyberg-Inan with Radu
    Cristescu
    The Ghosts in Our Classrooms, or:
    John Dewey Meets Ceaușescu
    The Promise and the Failures of Civic
    Education in Romania
    ISBN 3-89821-416-8

26 John B. Dunlop
    The 2002 Dubrovka and 2004 Beslan
    Hostage Crises
    A Critique of Russian Counter-Terrorism
    With a foreword by Donald N. Jensen
    ISBN 3-89821-608-X

27 Peter Koller
    Das touristische Potenzial von
    Kam''janec'–Podil's'kyj
    Eine fremdenverkehrsgeographische
    Untersuchung der Zukunftsperspektiven und
    Maßnahmenplanung zur
    Destinationsentwicklung des „ukrainischen
    Rothenburg"
    Mit einem Vorwort von Kristiane Klemm
    ISBN 3-89821-640-3

28 Françoise Daucé, Elisabeth Sieca-
    Kozlowski (Eds.)
    Dedovshchina in the Post-Soviet
    Military
    Hazing of Russian Army Conscripts in a
    Comparative Perspective
    With a foreword by Dale Herspring
    ISBN 3-89821-616-0

29 Florian Strasser
Zivilgesellschaftliche Einflüsse auf die Orange Revolution
Die gewaltlose Massenbewegung und die ukrainische Wahlkrise 2004
Mit einem Vorwort von Egbert Jahn
ISBN 3-89821-648-9

30 Rebecca S. Katz
The Georgian Regime Crisis of 2003-2004
A Case Study in Post-Soviet Media Representation of Politics, Crime and Corruption
ISBN 3-89821-413-3

31 Vladimir Kantor
Willkür oder Freiheit
Beiträge zur russischen Geschichtsphilosophie
Ediert von Dagmar Herrmann sowie mit einem Vorwort versehen von Leonid Luks
ISBN 3-89821-589-X

32 Laura A. Victoir
The Russian Land Estate Today
A Case Study of Cultural Politics in Post-Soviet Russia
With a foreword by Priscilla Roosevelt
ISBN 3-89821-426-5

33 Ivan Katchanovski
Cleft Countries
Regional Political Divisions and Cultures in Post-Soviet Ukraine and Moldova
With a foreword by Francis Fukuyama
ISBN 3-89821-558-X

34 Florian Mühlfried
Postsowjetische Feiern
Das Georgische Bankett im Wandel
Mit einem Vorwort von Kevin Tuite
ISBN 3-89821-601-2

35 Roger Griffin, Werner Loh, Andreas Umland (Eds.)
Fascism Past and Present, West and East
An International Debate on Concepts and Cases in the Comparative Study of the Extreme Right
With an afterword by Walter Laqueur
ISBN 3-89821-674-8

36 Sebastian Schlegel
Der „Weiße Archipel"
Sowjetische Atomstädte 1945-1991
Mit einem Geleitwort von Thomas Bohn
ISBN 3-89821-679-9

37 Vyacheslav Likhachev
Political Anti-Semitism in Post-Soviet Russia
Actors and Ideas in 1991-2003
Edited and translated from Russian by Eugene Veklerov
ISBN 3-89821-529-6

38 Josette Baer (Ed.)
Preparing Liberty in Central Europe
Political Texts from the Spring of Nations 1848 to the Spring of Prague 1968
With a foreword by Zdeněk V. David
ISBN 3-89821-546-6

39 Михаил Лукьянов
Российский консерватизм и реформа, 1907-1914
С предисловием Марка Д. Стейнберга
ISBN 3-89821-503-2

40 Nicola Melloni
Market Without Economy
The 1998 Russian Financial Crisis
With a foreword by Eiji Furukawa
ISBN 3-89821-407-9

41 Dmitrij Chmelnizki
Die Architektur Stalins
Bd. 1: Studien zu Ideologie und Stil
Bd. 2: Bilddokumentation
Mit einem Vorwort von Bruno Flierl
ISBN 3-89821-515-6

42 Katja Yafimava
Post-Soviet Russian-Belarussian Relationships
The Role of Gas Transit Pipelines
With a foreword by Jonathan P. Stern
ISBN 3-89821-655-1

43 Boris Chavkin
Verflechtungen der deutschen und russischen Zeitgeschichte
Aufsätze und Archivfunde zu den Beziehungen Deutschlands und der Sowjetunion von 1917 bis 1991
Ediert von Markus Edlinger sowie mit einem Vorwort versehen von Leonid Luks
ISBN 3-89821-756-6

44 *Anastasija Grynenko in Zusammenarbeit mit Claudia Dathe*
    Die Terminologie des Gerichtswesens der Ukraine und Deutschlands im Vergleich
    Eine übersetzungswissenschaftliche Analyse juristischer Fachbegriffe im Deutschen, Ukrainischen und Russischen
    Mit einem Vorwort von Ulrich Hartmann
    ISBN 3-89821-691-8

45 *Anton Burkov*
    The Impact of the European Convention on Human Rights on Russian Law
    Legislation and Application in 1996-2006
    With a foreword by Françoise Hampson
    ISBN 978-3-89821-639-5

46 *Stina Torjesen, Indra Overland (Eds.)*
    International Election Observers in Post-Soviet Azerbaijan
    Geopolitical Pawns or Agents of Change?
    ISBN 978-3-89821-743-9

47 *Taras Kuzio*
    Ukraine – Crimea – Russia
    Triangle of Conflict
    ISBN 978-3-89821-761-3

48 *Claudia Šabić*
    "Ich erinnere mich nicht, aber L'viv!"
    Zur Funktion kultureller Faktoren für die Institutionalisierung und Entwicklung einer ukrainischen Region
    Mit einem Vorwort von Melanie Tatur
    ISBN 978-3-89821-752-1

49 *Marlies Bilz*
    Tatarstan in der Transformation
    Nationaler Diskurs und Politische Praxis 1988-1994
    Mit einem Vorwort von Frank Golczewski
    ISBN 978-3-89821-722-4

50 *Марлен Ларюэль (ред.)*
    Современные интерпретации русского национализма
    ISBN 978-3-89821-795-8

51 *Sonja Schüler*
    Die ethnische Dimension der Armut
    Roma im postsozialistischen Rumänien
    Mit einem Vorwort von Anton Sterbling
    ISBN 978-3-89821-776-7

52 *Галина Кожевникова*
    Радикальный национализм в России и противодействие ему
    Сборник докладов Центра «Сова» за 2004-2007 гг.
    С предисловием Александра Верховского
    ISBN 978-3-89821-721-7

53 *Галина Кожевникова и Владимир Прибыловский*
    Российская власть в биографиях I
    Высшие должностные лица РФ в 2004 г.
    ISBN 978-3-89821-796-5

54 *Галина Кожевникова и Владимир Прибыловский*
    Российская власть в биографиях II
    Члены Правительства РФ в 2004 г.
    ISBN 978-3-89821-797-2

55 *Галина Кожевникова и Владимир Прибыловский*
    Российская власть в биографиях III
    Руководители федеральных служб и агентств РФ в 2004 г.
    ISBN 978-3-89821-798-9

56 *Ileana Petroniu*
    Privatisierung in Transformationsökonomien
    Determinanten der Restrukturierungs-Bereitschaft am Beispiel Polens, Rumäniens und der Ukraine
    Mit einem Vorwort von Rainer W. Schäfer
    ISBN 978-3-89821-790-3

57 *Christian Wipperfürth*
    Russland und seine GUS-Nachbarn
    Hintergründe, aktuelle Entwicklungen und Konflikte in einer ressourcenreichen Region
    ISBN 978-3-89821-801-6

58 *Togzhan Kassenova*
    From Antagonism to Partnership
    The Uneasy Path of the U.S.-Russian Cooperative Threat Reduction
    With a foreword by Christoph Bluth
    ISBN 978-3-89821-707-1

59 *Alexander Höllwerth*
    Das sakrale eurasische Imperium des Aleksandr Dugin
    Eine Diskursanalyse zum postsowjetischen russischen Rechtsextremismus
    Mit einem Vorwort von Dirk Uffelmann
    ISBN 978-3-89821-813-9

60 Олег Рябов
«Россия-Матушка»
Национализм, гендер и война в России XX века
С предисловием Елены Гощило
ISBN 978-3-89821-487-2

61 Ivan Maistrenko
Borot'bism
A Chapter in the History of the Ukrainian Revolution
With a new introduction by Chris Ford
Translated by George S. N. Luckyj with the assistance of Ivan L. Rudnytsky
ISBN 978-3-89821-697-5

62 Maryna Romanets
Anamorphosic Texts and Reconfigured Visions
Improvised Traditions in Contemporary Ukrainian and Irish Literature
ISBN 978-3-89821-576-3

63 Paul D'Anieri and Taras Kuzio (Eds.)
Aspects of the Orange Revolution I
Democratization and Elections in Post-Communist Ukraine
ISBN 978-3-89821-698-2

64 Bohdan Harasymiw in collaboration with Oleh S. Ilnytzkyj (Eds.)
Aspects of the Orange Revolution II
Information and Manipulation Strategies in the 2004 Ukrainian Presidential Elections
ISBN 978-3-89821-699-9

65 Ingmar Bredies, Andreas Umland and Valentin Yakushik (Eds.)
Aspects of the Orange Revolution III
The Context and Dynamics of the 2004 Ukrainian Presidential Elections
ISBN 978-3-89821-803-0

66 Ingmar Bredies, Andreas Umland and Valentin Yakushik (Eds.)
Aspects of the Orange Revolution IV
Foreign Assistance and Civic Action in the 2004 Ukrainian Presidential Elections
ISBN 978-3-89821-808-5

67 Ingmar Bredies, Andreas Umland and Valentin Yakushik (Eds.)
Aspects of the Orange Revolution V
Institutional Observation Reports on the 2004 Ukrainian Presidential Elections
ISBN 978-3-89821-809-2

68 Taras Kuzio (Ed.)
Aspects of the Orange Revolution VI
Post-Communist Democratic Revolutions in Comparative Perspective
ISBN 978-3-89821-820-7

69 Tim Bohse
Autoritarismus statt Selbstverwaltung
Die Transformation der kommunalen Politik in der Stadt Kaliningrad 1990-2005
Mit einem Geleitwort von Stefan Troebst
ISBN 978-3-89821-782-8

70 David Rupp
Die Rußländische Föderation und die russischsprachige Minderheit in Lettland
Eine Fallstudie zur Anwaltspolitik Moskaus gegenüber den russophonen Minderheiten im „Nahen Ausland" von 1991 bis 2002
Mit einem Vorwort von Helmut Wagner
ISBN 978-3-89821-778-1

71 Taras Kuzio
Theoretical and Comparative Perspectives on Nationalism
New Directions in Cross-Cultural and Post-Communist Studies
With a foreword by Paul Robert Magocsi
ISBN 978-3-89821-815-3

72 Christine Teichmann
Die Hochschultransformation im heutigen Osteuropa
Kontinuität und Wandel bei der Entwicklung des postkommunistischen Universitätswesens
Mit einem Vorwort von Oskar Anweiler
ISBN 978-3-89821-842-9

73 Julia Kusznir
Der politische Einfluss von Wirtschaftseliten in russischen Regionen
Eine Analyse am Beispiel der Erdöl- und Erdgasindustrie, 1992-2005
Mit einem Vorwort von Wolfgang Eichwede
ISBN 978-3-89821-821-4

74 Alena Vysotskaya
Russland, Belarus und die EU-Osterweiterung
Zur Minderheitenfrage und zum Problem der Freizügigkeit des Personenverkehrs
Mit einem Vorwort von Katlijn Malfliet
ISBN 978-3-89821-822-1

75 Heiko Pleines (Hrsg.)
Corporate Governance in postsozialistischen Volkswirtschaften
ISBN 978-3-89821-766-8

76 Stefan Ihrig
Wer sind die Moldawier?
Rumänismus versus Moldowanismus in Historiographie und Schulbüchern der Republik Moldova, 1991-2006
Mit einem Vorwort von Holm Sundhaussen
ISBN 978-3-89821-466-7

77 Galina Kozhevnikova in collaboration with Alexander Verkhovsky and Eugene Veklerov
Ultra-Nationalism and Hate Crimes in Contemporary Russia
The 2004-2006 Annual Reports of Moscow's SOVA Center
With a foreword by Stephen D. Shenfield
ISBN 978-3-89821-868-9

78 Florian Küchler
The Role of the European Union in Moldova's Transnistria Conflict
With a foreword by Christopher Hill
ISBN 978-3-89821-850-4

FORTHCOMING (MANUSCRIPT WORKING TITLES)

Stephanie Solowyda
Biography of Semen Frank
ISBN 3-89821-457-5

Margaret Dikovitskaya
Arguing with the Photographs
Russian Imperial Colonial Attitudes in Visual Culture
ISBN 3-89821-462-1

Sergei M. Plekhanov
Russian Nationalism in the Age of Globalization
ISBN 3-89821-484-2

Robert Pyrah
Cultural Memory and Identity
Literature, Criticism and the Theatre in Lviv - Lwow - Lemberg, 1918-1939 and in post-Soviet Ukraine
ISBN 3-89821-505-9

Andrei Rogatchevski
The National-Bolshevik Party
ISBN 3-89821-532-6

Zenon Victor Wasyliw
Soviet Culture in the Ukrainian Village
The Transformation of Everyday Life and Values, 1921-1928
ISBN 3-89821-536-9

Nele Sass
Das gegenkulturelle Milieu im postsowjetischen Russland
ISBN 3-89821-543-1

Julie Elkner
Maternalism versus Militarism
The Russian Soldiers' Mothers Committee
ISBN 3-89821-575-X

Alexandra Kamarowsky
Russia's Post-crisis Growth
ISBN 3-89821-580-6

Martin Friessnegg
Das Problem der Medienfreiheit in Russland seit dem Ende der Sowjetunion
ISBN 3-89821-588-1

Nikolaj Nikiforowitsch Borobow
Führende Persönlichkeiten in Russland vom 12. bis 20 Jhd.: Ein Lexikon
Aus dem Russischen übersetzt und herausgegeben von Eberhard Schneider
ISBN 3-89821-638-1

Martin Malek, Anna Schor-Tschudnowskaja
Tschetschenien und die Gleichgültigkeit Europas
Russlands Kriege und die Agonie der Idee der Menschenrechte
ISBN 3-89821-676-4

Andreas Langenohl
Political Culture and Criticism of Society
Intellectual Articulations in Post-Soviet Russia
ISBN 3-89821-709-6

Thomas Borén
Meeting Places in Transformation
ISBN 3-89821-739-6

Lars Löckner
Sowjetrussland in der Beurteilung der Emigrantenzeitung 'Rul', 1920-1924
ISBN 3-89821-741-8

Ekaterina Taratuta
The Red Line of Construction
Semantics and Mythology of a Siberian Heliopolis
ISBN 3-89821-742-6

Bernd Kappenberg
Zeichen setzen für Europa
Der Gebrauch europäischer lateinischer Sonderzeichen
in der deutschen Öffentlichkeit
ISBN 3-89821-749-3

Siegbert Klee, Martin Sandhop, Oxana
Schwajka, Andreas Umland
Elitenbildung in der Postsowjetischen
Ukraine
ISBN 978-389821-829-0

Natalya Ketenci
The effect of location on the performance of
Kazakhstani industrial enterprises in the
transition period
ISBN 978-389821-831-3

Quotes from reviews of SPPS volumes:

On vol. 1 – *The Implementation of the ECHR in Russia*: "Full of examples, experiences and valuable observations which could provide the basis for new strategies."

Diana Schmidt, *Неприкосновенный запас*, 2005

On vol. 2 – *Putins Russland*: "Wipperfürth draws attention to little known facts. For instance, the Russians have still more positive feelings towards Germany than to any other non-Slavic country."

Oldag Kaspar, *Süddeutsche Zeitung*, 2005

On vol. 3 – *Die Übernahme internationalen Rechts in die russische Rechtsordnung*: "Hussner's is an interesting, detailed and, at the same time, focused study which deals with all relevant aspects and contains insights into contemporary Russian legal thought."

Herbert Küpper, *Jahrbuch für Ostrecht*, 2005

On vol. 5 – *Квадратные метры, определяющие сознание*: „Meerovich provides a study that will be of considerable value to housing specialists and policy analysts."

Christina Varga-Harris, *Slavic Review*, 2006

On vol. 6 – *New Directions in Russian International Studies*: "A helpful step in the direction of an overdue dialogue between Western and Russian IR scholarly communities."

Diana Schmidt, *Europe-Asia Studies*, 2006

On vol. 8 – *Nation-Building and Minority Politics in Post-Socialist States*: "Galbreath's book is an admirable and craftsmanlike piece of work, and should be read by all specialists interested in the Baltic area."

Andrejs Plakans, *Slavic Review*, 2007

On vol. 9 – *Народы Кавказа в Вооружённых силах СССР*: "In this superb new book, Bezugolnyi skillfully fashions an accurate and candid record of how and why the Soviet Union mobilized and employed the various ethnic groups in the Caucasus region in the Red Army's World War II effort."

David J. Glantz, *Journal of Slavic Military Studies*, 2006

On vol. 10 – *Русское Национальное Единство*: "Pribylovskii's and Likhachev's work is likely to remain the definitive study of the Russian National Unity for a very long time."

Mischa Gabowitsch, *e-Extreme*, 2006

On vol. 13 – *The Politicization of Russian Orthodoxy*: "Mitrofanova's book is a fascinating study which raises important questions about the type of national ideology that will come to predominate in the new Russia."

Zoe Knox, *Europe-Asia Studies*, 2006

On vol. 14 – *Aleksandr Solzhenitsyn and the Modern Russo-Jewish Question*: "Larson has written a well-balanced survey of Solzhenitsyn's writings on Russian-Jewish relations."

Nikolai Butkevich, *e-Extreme*, 2006

On vol. 16 – *Der russische Sonderweg?:* "Luks's remarkable knowledge of the history of this wide territory from the Elbe to the Pacific Ocean and his life experience give his observations a particular sharpness and his judgements an exceptional weight."

Peter Krupnikow, *Mitteilungen aus dem baltischen Leben*, 2006

On vol. 17 – *История «Мёртвой воды»:* "Moroz provides one of the best available surveys of Russian neo-paganism."

Mischa Gabowitsch, *e-Extreme*, 2006

On vol. 18 – *Этническая и религиозная интолерантность в российских СМИ:* "A constructive contribution to a crucial debate about media-endorsed intolerance which has once again flared up in Russia."

Mischa Gabowitsch, *e-Extreme*, 2006

On vol. 25 – *The Ghosts in Our Classroom:* "Freyberg-Inan's well-researched and incisive monograph, balanced and informed about Romanian education in general, should be required reading for those Eurocrats who have shaped Romanian spending priorities since 2000."

Tom Gallagher, *Slavic Review*, 2006

On vol. 26 – *The 2002 Dubrovka and 2004 Beslan Hostage Crises:* "Dunlop's analysis will help to draw Western attention to the plight of those who have suffered by these terrorist acts, and the importance, for all Russians, of uncovering the truth of about what happened."

Amy Knight, *Times Literary Supplement*, 2006

On vol. 29 – *Zivilgesellschaftliche Einflüsse auf die Orange Revolution:* „Strasser's study constitutes an outstanding empirical analysis and well-grounded location of the subject within theory."

Heiko Pleines, *Osteuropa*, 2006

On vol. 34 – *Postsowjetische Feiern:* "Mühlfried's book contains not only a solid ethnographic study, but also points at some problems emerging from Georgia's prevalent understanding of culture."

Godula Kosack, *Anthropos*, 2007

On vol. 35 – *Fascism Past and Present, West and East:* "Committed students will find much of interest in these sometimes barbed exchanges."

Robert Paxton, *Journal of Global History*, 2007

On vol. 37 – *Political Anti-Semitism in Post-Soviet Russia:* "Likhachev's book serves as a reliable compendium and a good starting point for future research on post-Soviet xenophobia and ultra-nationalist politics, with their accompanying anti-Semitism."

Kathleen Mikkelson, *Demokratizatsiya*, 2007

Series Subscription

Please enter my subscription to the series *Soviet and Post-Soviet Politics and Society*, ISSN 1614-3515, as follows:

❏ complete series   OR   ❏ English-language titles
                                                       ❏ German-language titles
                                                       ❏ Russian-language titles

starting with
❏ volume # 1
❏ volume # ___
    ❏ please also include the following volumes: #___, ___, ___, ___, ___, ___, ___
❏ the next volume being published
    ❏ please also include the following volumes: #___, ___, ___, ___, ___, ___, ___

❏ 1 copy per volume   OR   ❏ ___ copies per volume

Subscription within Germany:

You will receive every volume at 1st publication at the regular bookseller's price – incl. s & h and VAT.
Payment:
❏ Please bill me for every volume.
❏ Lastschriftverfahren: Ich/wir   ermächtige(n)   Sie   hiermit   widerruflich,   den Rechnungsbetrag je Band von meinem/unserem folgendem Konto einzuziehen.

Kontoinhaber: _____Kreditinstitut: _____
Kontonummer: _____Bankleitzahl:_____

International Subscription:

Payment (incl. s & h and VAT) in advance for
❏ 10 volumes/copies (€ 319.80)   ❏ 20 volumes/copies (€ 599.80)
❏ 40 volumes/copies (€ 1,099.80)
Please send my books to:

NAME_____DEPARTMENT_____
ADDRESS _____
POST/ZIP CODE_____COUNTRY_____
TELEPHONE _____EMAIL_____

date/signature_____

A hint for librarians in the former Soviet Union: Your academic library might be eligible to receive free-of-cost scholarly literature from Germany via the German Research Foundation. For Russian-language information on this program, see
        http://www.dfg.de/forschungsfoerderung/formulare/download/12_54.pdf.

Please fax to: **0511 / 262 2201 (+49 511 262 2201)**
or mail to: *ibidem*-Verlag, Julius-Leber-Weg 11, D-30457 Hannover,Germany
or send an e-mail: ibidem@ibidem-verlag.de

***ibidem*-**Verlag
Melchiorstr. 15
D-70439 Stuttgart

info@ibidem-verlag.de

www.ibidem-verlag.de
www.edition-noema.de
www.autorenbetreuung.de

www.ingramcontent.com/pod-product-compliance
Lightning Source LLC
Chambersburg PA
CBHW071941240426
43669CB00048B/2480